HYPNOTIC
LEADERSHIP

HYPNOTIC
LEADERSHIP

Leaders, Followers, and the Loss of Self

MICHA POPPER

Westport, Connecticut
London

Library of Congress Cataloging-in-Publication Data

Popper, Micha, 1947–
    Hypnotic leadership : leaders, followers, and the loss of self / Micha Popper.
        p.   cm.
    Includes bibliographical references and index.
    ISBN 0–275–97138–4 (alk. paper)
    1. Leadership.   2. Control (Psychology).   3. Dominance (Psychology).
    4. Brainwashing.   I. Title.
    BF637.L4P65   2001
    303.3′4—dc21   00–064942

British Library Cataloguing in Publication Data is available.

Library of Congress Catalog Card Number: 00–064942
ISBN: 0–275–97138–4

First published in 2001

Praeger Publishers, 88 Post Road West, Westport, CT 06881
An imprint of Greenwood Publishing Group, Inc.
www.praeger.com

Printed in the United States of America

The paper used in this book complies with the
Permanent Paper Standard issued by the National
Information Standards Organization (Z39.48–1984).

10 9 8 7 6 5 4 3 2 1

In memory of my father
Dr. Tuvia (Tony) Popper

Contents

Introduction   ix

1   The Spark—Hypnotic Leaders   1
    Charles Manson   1
    Jim Jones   6
    Adolf Hitler   10
    Analysis of the Leadership Phenomenon   12

2   The Fuel—Hypnotized Followers   33
    The Tale of a Feeble-Minded Gardener   33
    "You Have a Mantle, You Shall Be Our Leader"   36

3   The Fire—Leaders, Followers, and Circumstances   43
    The Meeting of the Spark, the Fuel, and the Oxygen   43
    The Conflagration   51
    Forces That Fan the Flame or Cool It   66
    The Faust-Mephistopheles Myth   75

Some Thoughts in Conclusion   81
    Leadership and Influence   82
    Leadership and Circles of Influence   83
    More about the Development of Leaders   90
    Some Further Reflections   98

Glossary   103

Notes   107

Index   117

Introduction

In 1978, Jim Jones stood on a small platform, looking with clouded eyes at the scores of believers drinking in his every word, and in a trembling voice, choking back his tears, said, "You'll never be loved again like I love you."

A few hours later, the world heard with shock that his followers (911, including children) had poisoned themselves to death because "we don't want any part of this world," in Jones's words. A few minutes after the mass suicide, the deathly silence that enveloped the forest clearing in Jonestown, Guiana, was shattered by two shots. Jim Jones, the idolized leader, had shot his young girlfriend, Ann Moore, and then shot himself.

This event was a horror not only because of the appalling act itself, but also because of the "terrifying" fact, as Reston[1] put it in one of his studies, "that Jones's believers were sane people in every accepted clinical sense; in fact, these people were completely normal." Furthermore, people who testified after the case that they belonged to the cult but had been away from Jonestown at the time of the suicide asserted that "the members of the cult were far from robots, as might be expected."[2] The evidence of some of the cult members who survived because they had been away from Jonestown at the time emphasizes the amazing power of Jones's influence. One of the surviving members wept bitterly and surprised the person trying to console him by saying, "I wanted to die with my friends. I wanted to die with Jim. I wanted to do what they did."[3]

The case of Jones and his believers is an example of "leadership in action." Jones is an example of a leader whose influence is immensely powerful—to the point of death! Can leadership be more powerful? This is the ultimate in leadership.

Most people would agree that it is hard to think of people such as Jones in terms of leadership. We are used to thinking of leadership as a positive phenomenon and seeing it in idealized terms (particularly in Anglo-American culture). Every large bookstore has shelves loaded with books about visionary social leaders who shaped cultures and led their society to a better future, biographies of leaders who "made it." For example, the biographies of such leaders of industry as Lee Iaccoca, president of Chrysler, or Harold Ginin of ITT, were sold by the million, turning these leaders into culture heroes and models for imitation.

The human tendency to attribute to leaders great, almost superhuman, powers to generate development and change will be discussed in this book. This tendency is so strong that we often forget (too often, as modern history has shown) that leadership can also be dangerous and destructive.

This book deals with an aspect of leadership to which there is surprisingly little reference in the psychological literature. There have been psychobiographies of destructive leaders such as Hitler, but the *phenomenon* itself, with its dark, even pathological, sides has barely been touched on. By pathological I do not mean that it can happen only among deviant populations. The case of Nazi Germany is horrifying evidence that in certain circumstances even normal people can be caught up in this phenomenon, and in fact, play a vital part in maintaining its existence.

In this book, leadership is compared to fire. Three components are needed to start a fire and keep it going: spark—the leader,

fuel—the followers, and oxygen to feed the flames—the circumstances. Each of these components is necessary; the important
point is the combination of the three. This book analyzes the dynamics among the leader, the followers, and the circumstances. In
my view, the dynamics of leadership cannot be understood without dealing with these three elements, and the professional literature has hitherto stressed the weight of the leader at the expense of
the other elements.

I should state at the outset that this book deals with extreme
forms of leadership, where the fire burns most intensely. Therefore,
the question of generalization naturally arises: Can we deduce
from such extreme situations to less extreme cases? Could Jim
Jones's story have occurred only among certain uneducated populations with a strong sense of deprivation? Could a leader such as
Hitler have developed and flourished only in the context of a German society with specific characteristics,[4] or could a phenomenon
of this kind develop in any society in times of severe crisis? Or are
there perhaps some societies that are more immune than others to
such dangers?

The question of generalization arises in the context of many theoretical discussions. Some of the better known theories that have
influenced Western thinking and culture were developed from a
very small number of cases, which would not have passed any statistical test as a basis for drawing conclusions and making generalizations. The most famous example of this is the work of Freud. He
based his theories on his observations of a small number of clients,
who were not a representative sample of the population at large (or
even of the population of Austria), and certainly not of its emotional and intellectual abilities. (There are some who say that his
theory was based on clients who could be defined as people with
pathological personalities.)[5] Nevertheless, therapists use his theoretical concepts with a large degree of generalization. Furthermore,
these concepts have taken root in everyday language, and terms
such as *defense mechanisms, repression, denial,* and *rationalization* are
heard in conversations among people with no pretensions to being
psychologists. The purpose of such a discussion at the theoretical

level is not to offer statistical evidence but to focus on a phenomenon that has such sharp emotional expressions that only extreme examples can show it clearly.

One point of departure for this discussion is to distinguish between leadership in everyday life—which exists in almost every human relationship, whether it be a teacher and his students, a manager and his staff, or, most commonly, parents and children—and leadership in extreme situations such as crisis situations. Can these everyday leadership relations teach us anything about leadership in crisis situations? We must bear in mind that it is not just the leader we are talking about but also the followers and an unfamiliar and threatening situation. Will these two components behave as usual? Will they have the same expectations? The psychological condition of all the participants in an extreme situation seems to change so much that one wonders whether the criteria for analysis of leadership in routine times are relevant.

One of the assumptions derived from my observation of crisis situations is that process-oriented psychological explanations, those known as psychodynamic explanations, are more relevant than others (as I will explain below). This impression was strengthened when I watched hundreds of youths filling the square where Israeli Prime Minister Yitzhak Rabin was assassinated. Many of them wept and spoke of "losing a father." Longing for a father is one of the better-known psychodynamic explanations of longing for a leader.

The image of the leader as a father was presented by Freud back in the 1930s: "People have a strong need for authority," wrote Freud, "authority that we can admire, before which we can bow, by which we are governed. We have learned the source of this need from the psychology of the individual. It is the longing for a father that everyone feels from his early childhood on."[6]

Thus, according to Freud, leaders represent the father at the unconscious level. The emotional attraction to leaders and the surrender to their authority provides a solution to conflicts and to powerful emotional tensions. Just as identification with the father solves the oedipal conflict, identification with the leader figure brings release from stress. According to the noted researcher on leadership, psychoanalyst Kets de Vries,[7] this emotional function of the leader can create euphoria in his followers, releasing guilt feelings created by various prohibitions.

Psychodynamic explanations on leader-follower relations of the type suggested by Freud and Kets de Vries pay little attention to the contents of the messages or the quality of the ideas represented by the leaders.[8] Their influence is explained only through unconscious processes centered on the classic psychodynamic concepts of projection and transference. "Projection," according to the *Dictionary of Psychoanalysis*,[9] is a process whereby certain aspects of the self, such as desires and impulses, are located in an object outside the self. This process is mostly related to a previous psychological mechanism, denial. The term "transference" was originally used to describe the process whereby the client transferred to the therapist emotions whose source was in figures from the past (usually the client's parents). These two concepts, projection and transference, are the basis of the explanation for the regressive psychological situation that arises in crisis situations. There is a tendency for the followers to "merge" totally with the leader, which Lindholm[10] called self loss. The effect of the crisis situation is supported by historical evidence that is more than incidental. For example, Hertzber,[11] who analyzed the rise to power of thirty-five dictators, found that all of them took over during crises. My assumption is that relations with leaders who are perceived by their followers as "hypnotic" are connected with the loss of autonomous reasoning, loss of the self, as in hypnosis.

Another point worth thinking about concerns the fact that psychology, in trying to be "scientific," has generally treated leadership as a value-free phenomenon.[12] Scholars presumed to find some order in the actual processes by which leaders exerted their influence. However, as some writers have pointed out, particularly in recent years, a discipline that claims to be scientific should also study the *directions* of phenomena, particularly those that have social significance, otherwise the link between research and reality becomes tenuous. It is true that a few studies, such as Zimbardo's[13] classic investigation of the limits of obedient behavior (which will be described below), added not only findings but also food for thought regarding human nature in certain circumstances. I venture to claim that this book, too, will stimulate thought and add new points of view. That is why I chose as the epigraph for this book Thomas Hardy's words: "If a way to be better there be, it lies in taking a full look at the worst." The readers, of course, will draw their own conclusions on my observations. At all events, the thoughts described here were what determined the structure of this book.

Chapter 1, "The Spark—Hypnotic Leaders," opens with descriptions of three such leaders, presented in rising order of influence. Charles Manson, leader of a small group numbering a few dozen people; Jim Jones, leader of hundreds; and Adolf Hitler, leader of millions. I chose these men because they were clearly destructive leaders who merited the title "hypnotic," and I chose to introduce them in this order for the purpose of discussing the ripple effect. Manson's influence might be perceived as the case of a small, random group of people gathered around a weird man who answered their special needs. However, when the circles of "hypnotic influence" extend to millions of people, this calls for more fundamental arguments, though we may still learn from the possible similarities (or differences) in these cases. Although the leaders themselves are only one ingredient in the mixture (the spark that lights the fire), I have described them at some length because I found it necessary to emphasize the emotional aspect. People reading in literature (of any kind) descriptions of emotions such as sadness, loneliness, happiness or fear can usually connect with these descriptions and understand them out of their own associations of emotional experiences. The emotions described in this book, however, are so singular that it is doubtful whether most people can draw on any personal association to help them understand. These psychological phenomena are hard to demonstrate in formal writing, so I have used many examples to assist me in describing the obsession to be a leader. For some of the leaders, it is a struggle for life, which explains the intensity of the spark.

I gained an inkling of the ambition that becomes an obsession when reading an interview with a well-known actor at a theater that was threatened with closure. The actor gave a graphic description of his elation when he stood at the center of the stage and of the emptiness that enveloped him when he walked out of the dressing room into the deserted streets, with no outlet for his emotions. Only the knowledge that there would be another play the next day gave him the strength to face this emptiness. "This is my life," he said, "if they close the theater, I have nothing to live for. I'm prepared to give up my salary as long as I can go on acting." Other actors who were interviewed at that time said that the truly great actors are those who feel that acting is "their real lives." This is how many leaders feel about the position of leadership. Although the motivation of actors and leaders does not necessarily come from the same sources, the need to be in the center of the stage, to be the object of attention, is cardinal. Hitler wrote about this explicitly. He saw struggle, in general, and the struggle for leadership, in particular, as a source of life. This feeling was shared by Jones and Manson, as will be shown in the book; in fact, it is a feeling shared by many others, including leaders who are not necessarily destructive. Churchill described it, so did Woodrow Wilson, and even superficial observation of the behavior of leaders cannot fail to show the level of energy and vitality they display when they are the center of attention. The word "vitality" is most pertinent, because it stems from the Latin *vita*, meaning life, and this is the meaning of leadership for some of the most outstanding leaders, as it certainly was for the leaders described in this book.

Furthermore, the biographies of leaders are important for understanding the specific psychological profile of "hypnotic" leaders. The hypnotic power of the leaders described is connected with a specific psychological profile that evolves out of their personal history. It is important to understand the nuances of this psychological profile, because everyone undergoes psychological experiences, which are defined by Aberbach[14] as trauma. According to Aberbach, the struggle with such experiences becomes a driving force. The argument will be presented that, in crisis situations, a rare meeting occurs between the collective trauma and the personal trauma experienced by the leader. But, says Aberbach, that same leader has accumulated personal experience of struggling with trauma (he refers to this experience as "schooling"). In a given crisis situation, whose psychological components are well known to the leader, he both understands the nuances of the crisis from his own experiences and conveys the sense that he can cope with it. All this reinforces the conditions in which the leader can easily become a "vehicle for the followers' projections and transferences."

Chapter 2, "The Fuel—Hypnotized Followers," deals with the object of the hypnosis, namely the followers. In this chapter, I discuss the basic, primary tendency to be hypnotized by leaders and attempt to demonstrate the process of longing for a leader. This longing has been described by various scholars, among them the psychoanalyst Erich Fromm, who claimed that it is so ingrained that people lose the wish to be autonomous; that is why he named his famous book *Escape from Freedom*.[15] However, critics of Fromm and others in the psychoanalytic stream labeled their arguments as universal, saying that their analyses left no room for diverse cultural aspects and circumstances, which Hofstede,[16] a researcher of cultures, felicitously described as "the software of the mind." These scholars demonstrate, for example, that cultures differ in their attitude toward authority and their ability to tolerate uncertainty—characteristics that are certainly significant in crisis situations and should be taken into account in analyzing the "flare-up."

Chapter 3, "The Fire—Leaders, Followers, and Circumstances," deals with the actual meeting of the components that create the fire and, as mentioned above, is the core of this book in terms of the fundamental argument. This chapter was rewritten several times because I discovered that my argument was complicated and hard to explain. Furthermore, for someone like me, who was strictly socialized to a method of writing based on fact presentation, detailed descriptions, quantitative values, and so forth, it is hard to write about phenomena whose explanation is highly intuitive. But the fact is that even researchers who devoted their entire lives to the study of phenomena such as the Holocaust do not agree among themselves on what brought it about and how it developed, despite the mounds of data and evidence they have collected. For example, as recently as 1996, Daniel Goldhagen, a young professor from Harvard, in a book entitled *Hitler's Willing Executioners* (New York: Alfred Knopf), claimed that the Germans' brutal treatment of the Jews was not just a matter of carrying out orders. It was "enthusiastic action" beyond the formal order. These acts sprang from feelings that went beyond the duty to obey the orders of a certain regime, no matter how arbitrary. This argument was sharply criticized, but it also gained support from some researchers; what they all had in common was thorough knowledge of the history of that period. I cite this example for two reasons, one, to show that there are phenomena, particularly those involving extreme emotions, that are hard to explain in the usual terms of scholarship, and even experienced and careful researchers cannot agree as to their causes. The other reason is that I wish to make it perfectly clear that I am not attempting to join the researchers and interpreters of a phenomenon like Nazi Germany. I have tried to do something much less pretentious and restrict myself to the discussion of "charismatic leadership": to characterize a phenomenon that causes "an emotional effect of identification to the extent of loss of autonomous sense of direction and control." In formulating it to myself this way, I could hardly ignore the historical example of Nazi Germany, but I want to stress that I refer to it here as an illustration of charismatic leadership at its extreme and not as the historical analysis of a period. The attempt to describe Hitler's influence is an attempt to demonstrate psychological explanations for a phenomenon that is hard to explain by any rational criterion. It seems to me that this formulation of the sentence clarifies how hard and vulnerable to criticism this task is.

From this point of departure, I took some concepts that seem to be central in the analysis of "hypnotic charismatic leadership" and tried to show how they are expressed in practice. For example, I learned that it is hard to show the influence of cultural codes on behavior. It is hard to show in concrete terms what a cultural code is and even harder to show how such a code influences the thinking and behavior of a given population. To demonstrate this, I used the post-Mephistophelian myth as a concrete expression of the influence of cultural codes in Germany. It should be noted that this is just an example, not the entire explanation.

Thus, Chapter 3 presents the concepts that I consider central in the analysis of "hypnotic charismatic" leadership. That is all I claim to do in this book: to present concepts that can help us to identify the dangerous phenomena related to charismatic leadership. Therefore, the book focuses more on concepts and questions, and does not claim to give definite answers, though I naturally hope that these concepts and questions will sharpen the sensitivity and understanding of the complexity of the phenomenon.

In the last chapter, "Some Thoughts in Conclusion," I return to some subjects that I felt required further discussion or that seemed important in providing an overall perspective for evaluation of leaders. In particular, I expanded on the distinction between "good" and "bad" leaders who are defined by Howell[17] as "personalized charismatic leaders" and "socialized charismatic leaders." The literature barely discusses the developmental processes at the basis of this distinction. To the best of my knowledge, this discussion in the developmental context is the first of its kind.

Finally, a few personal words: Writing a book of this kind is like throwing various ingredients into a pot until they form some kind of a stew. Many people contributed to this book, some of them without knowing it. Perhaps it was an article I read that gave me insight or the fascinating story of someone I met by chance in a restaurant or something said by a student in a lecture. Experiences such as these played a significant part in the development of this book, and perhaps of every book. From this point of view, the people who contributed indirectly to this book are too numerous to mention and to thank individually. Nevertheless, I wish to express my gratitude to some writers whose works were the initial stimulus for this endeavor. An article in *Leadership Quarterly* by Professor Boas Shamir of the Hebrew University of Jerusalem, on alternative explanations for the development of "charismatic relations," first stimulated my thinking in this direction, and traces of it can be found in the book. Professor Kets de Vries of the School of Management in Fontainebleu, particularly his book *Prisoners of Leadership*, added greatly to my understanding of leadership processes from a psychodynamic perspective. In writing about hypnotic leaders, I was helped enormously by Professor Charles Lindholm of Boston University with his book on charisma. The book *Cultures and Organizations*, by Professor Gerte Hofstede of Limburg University in Holland, helped me to understand the cultural context. A book by Dr. Rivka Shechter of Tel Aviv University on the theological elements of the Third Reich contributed a great deal to my understanding of German culture. *Organizational Culture and Leadership* by Professor Edgar Schein of MIT in Boston, has for years helped me to understand the relationship between leadership and culture. Finally, the monumental books by Professors James McGregor Burns, *Leadership*, and Bernard Bass, *Leadership and Performance Beyond Expectations*, are what motivated me to delve more deeply into this intriguing area of leadership. It goes without saying that every writer listed in the notes contributed in some way to the creation of this book, but I am particularly indebted to those mentioned here. Today, I understand better than ever the Chinese saying that writing a book is like bearing a child; these children, in my opinion, possess special merit.

I would like to say a few words about the style of writing. I faced a dilemma: On the one hand, I believe that leadership, charisma, and the other topics discussed in this book are of concern to the public at large. On the other hand, a deep understanding of them requires some knowledge of the concepts and ways of thinking prevalent in the behavioral sciences. How does one write a book that will arouse interest and thought among as wide an audience as possible without the risk of overpopularization of highly complex phenomena? Believing that the messages and the contents of this kind of book merit discussion beyond sectarian academic frameworks, I sought a middle path, using many concrete illustrations and writing as clearly as possible.

Finally, I wish to thank all those who invested efforts, time, and thought in helping me directly with various aspects of the book: my family, my friends, and my students. In addition to my family and friends, who gave me their unstinting support and advice in the process of developing ideas for this book, I wish to express special thanks to three people: to Dr. Reuven Gal and Professor Boas Shamir, for their helpful and insightful comments on the early version of the book, and to Hazel Arieli, for her linguistic sensitivity and intuition in translating and editing the manuscript.

CHAPTER 1

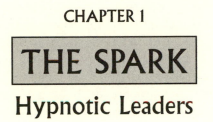

THE SPARK
Hypnotic Leaders

If a way to be better there be, it lies in taking a full look at the worst.
Thomas Hardy

CHARLES MANSON

Charles Manson headed a murderous group known as "the Manson family," which slaughtered a number of people at a party in Los Angeles at the end of the 1960s, including the beautiful actress Sharon Tate, wife of the famous film director Roman Polansky. The Manson family aroused a great deal of interest among the American public because its members, except for Manson himself, came from wealthy, educated families who were typical representatives of the upper middle classes. These were not miserable and destitute outcasts with nothing to lose, but young people "born with a silver spoon in their mouths," people with excellent education and a guaranteed future. The question as to what caused them to follow Charles Manson or, rather, to surrender themselves completely to such a man, was not just a matter of anecdote or gossip, but a sociological question touching on the foundations of the American education. The number of articles and books written on the subject, press and TV interviews, and debates of all kinds indicate that this was not seen as just "another murder," the like of which takes place every day somewhere in the United States. This was an attack on the very foundations of the American dream.

Charles Manson was born in 1934 and was a few years older than his followers (the "family" operated between 1967 and 1969). Unlike his followers, he came from a lower-class family. In fact, his family situation was chaotic: Abandonment and illegitimacy were the outstanding characteristics of his childhood. He never knew his father, was abandoned by his mother in infancy, and was raised by distant relatives, who shifted him from family to family. He never knew a permanent or warm home. The longest period he spent in any one place was with his grandmother, who was extremely rigid and authoritarian. His personality was dominated by his sense of abandonment. As he described it to his biographer: "I was an outlaw from birth. . . . Rejection, more than love and acceptance, has been a part of my life since birth."[1] In a press interview, Manson said, "The man whose seed created me lost all contact with my mother. I got the name Manson from William Manson, who was my mother's boyfriend at the time. My mother had neither the desire nor the ability to take the responsibility for raising me. You might say I was a child that nobody wanted."[2] The abandonment and neglect experienced by Manson in his childhood were given horrifying expression in the story he told in that same interview: "One day, while my mother was sitting in a café with me in her arms, the waitress complimented her on the cute baby. My mother replied that she would sell me for a glass of beer. And she did. It took a few days until one of my cousins found me and brought me home." Even if the story is completely fictitious, the fact that he invented it is a key to understanding Manson's personality and self-perception.

Manson longed so much for love that the thing most threatening to him was *the betrayal of love*, and this characteristic would become a central motif in his life. In practice, hate and rejection of intimate feelings characterized his behavior toward people in general and toward his followers in particular—his followers who admired but did not love him. The sadistic elements in his personality first appeared at the age of thirteen in his boys' school, where he was accused of cruel behavior by the seniors. At the age of sixteen, he was sent to prison, where he met people whose identity had been formed by a life of crime, and he adopted this persona for himself. But here, too, he failed. He turned out to be a poor thief; he was caught and jailed again. When he was released, his wife left him. He was arrested again for robbery and sentenced to ten years in jail. And thus, once again, Manson found himself deserted and abandoned by everyone he knew in the outside world.

In jail, he found the closest substitute to a home in the end, and there he spent most of his adult life. In fact, he did not want to be released when he finished serving his sentence. Life outside prison was a hardship for him. As he described it to his biographer: "I found myself sleeping in filthy rooms, wondering how I would pay the rent on time and how I would find food for the next day."[3]

The circumstances and atmosphere of that period (1967), particularly in San Francisco, helped him to readjust to life outside prison and become accepted by his followers as "head of a family" and, above all, to remodel himself and acquire his self-image as "family leader."

At that time in San Francisco, more than anywhere else in the United States, poverty was not considered shameful. People slept in the streets undisturbed, and love, sex, and drugs were free. Nobody paid attention to Manson's past. His hippie appearance and his talent for playing the guitar enabled him to live even better than he had lived before in other places. He was then, as he told his biographer, "quite a happy man." By his account, it was his "students" who taught him all the practices that were later attributed to him, such as the use of drugs and LSD, while his influence on them was in the perception that was so characteristic of his attitude toward life, summarized in the following words: "The door is not the way out. The way out is when you don't want to go out any more—only then are you free."

The message, that a person can release himself spiritually, subjectively, fell on fertile soil. His students, especially in light of the background from which they came, received this message eagerly, as described by one of them: "The man himself (Manson) and the journey he had undergone through rejection and suffering to spiritual rebirth was an example to them."[4]

Manson, in fact, reconstructed for the group members the process that he himself had undergone. According to his beliefs, in order to achieve the required spontaneity, people had to experience "psychological and spiritual death, that would break every independent individual and leave him with a dead head."[5]

Manson called this "reprogramming," a process which, according to him, entailed "peeling off all the false masks." This approach was expressed in the books he read and in the attitudes he adopted under the influence of these books. For example, he was strongly influenced by Eric Berne's book *Games People Play*, in which Berne discusses various types of children. In the typology he suggests, one of the types is "the pure child." The idea of the pure child, the creation of a such a child, was one of Manson's dreams. A child "free of parents," a child "who lives the present, the moment, and never wonders where he comes from and what he was."[6] In a press interview, he said that he used to explain to his followers that life had taught him that "a person has to forget yesterday and who he was before. He should not develop hopes about what tomorrow will bring. I explained to them that they should not pin their hopes on one person because sooner or later that person will let you down. Also, I agreed with them that they had to get out of the rat race because they would soon become greedier."[7]

Talking to his biographer about his hopes for the family, Manson quoted the sermon that he was in the habit of delivering regularly to his "disciples": "Let us leave aside the remains of our ego, let us free ourselves of the garbage that our parents threw at us, let us just be ourselves, such strong individuals, until we all become one."[8]

Indeed, the entire lifestyle of the family was present-oriented. The members of the family called each other by nicknames; they did not know their friends' real names or anything about their past. The only one whose life story and real name they knew was Manson. Manson's indoctrination succeeded in generating feelings of joy and happiness in the family members. As one of them described it: "It was love that flowed through your body like thick syrup in your veins, warming wherever it went, making you so 'one' with the person you were with that you'd have laid down your own life for him or her, and it would not have mattered because you were so 'one' that the distinctions between the two of you hardly existed any more."[9]

Manson had two outstanding characteristics: inner emptiness, from which he found escape in the power he accumulated, and the remarkable ability to identify loneliness in others. He needed the group no less than the group needed him. In fact, projecting his feelings onto the group saved him from thoughts of escape and death. As he described it: "I often had the urge to get my things together and head for unknown places, but I was so caught up with those kids and the role I played in their lives, to leave them would have been like ripping my heart out. Something inside me needed them, more than they thought they needed me."[10]

And, thus, the preoccupation with release through death was replaced by the theme of giving, of redeeming tortured souls. But death lurked beneath these rationalizations and found its expression when the cracks appeared. The first signs of this, as usual, were signs of paranoia. In the state of anxiety (in the clinical sense) that overpowered Manson shortly before the murders, he began to rationalize the fear as an expression of vitality. The family began to live like a pack of wolves sunk in total paranoia. And total paranoia, according to Manson at that time, was "total awareness."[11] They began to carry knives, and Manson himself carried a "magic sword." They began to travel in roundabout ways, driving very quickly, they practiced stalking, and gradually internalized the feeling that they were being hunted. The external pressure and Manson's inner state put terrible pressure on the group dynamics, and they reached such a highly charged psychological state that they had to do something to release the pressure, otherwise the group would break up. Manson began to picture a catalyzing act that would destroy the forces of evil and darkness so that a new era could commence. The murders they planned gained legitimacy from the inner logic that developed in the family. However, underneath all the psychological explanations and processes that created legitimacy for the terrible act, lurked hatred, and the worst of all was Manson's hatred: "This fucking society tears all my loves away from me, I'll show them, they [outside society] have turned us into animals, I will free the animals, I'll give them so much fucking fear that people will be afraid to go out of their houses."[12]

Naturally, Manson's words of hatred did not fall on deaf ears, because this was what had attracted the group to him in the first place. To them, he represented the opposite of their hated parents— successful, middle-class, career-minded people, who were so absorbed in themselves that they had given their children an unbearable experience of marginality. Manson was a counteracting force to their parents' paralyzing power, but they perceived this force as their own. For the first time in their lives, they felt omnipotent, strong, capable of shattering, breaking, and destroying. No power could match them when they were "one" and near Manson. However, Manson had a new theme: This time, rather than being abandoned again, Manson was prepared to kill, to destroy. It was much easier than being abandoned once more. As soon as this awareness and these feelings became rooted in the family spirit, the brutal murders that took place a few days later were no longer a red line not to be crossed.

JIM JONES

Jim Jones was a lonely man. Loneliness was part of his daily experience. Even when he was surrounded by people, this feeling did not leave him entirely. When he was not with other people, the bitter sense of loneliness was often accompanied by boundless rage and hostility. "I was ready to kill by the end of third grade," said Jones to a journalist who interviewed him in jail where he was imprisoned for robbery. "I mean, I was so aggressive and hostile, I was ready to kill. Nobody gave me any, any understanding. I am standing there alone. Always was alone."[13]

Jim Jones, like many other charismatic leaders (as we shall see later in this book), was an outsider, a deviant boy in his class. He grew up in a small town in Indiana. His father, a disabled, bitter man and a drinker, died when Jim was a child. His story is typical of many of the more charismatic leaders in human history.

Jim's mother, a factory worker, was nonconformist in her attitudes and behaviors and had artistic inclinations. She saw herself as a woman with "the soul of an artist" and led what she believed to be a bohemian life. She drank, smoked marihuana, and apparently spent a lot of time outside the house. Jim remained completely alone at home for hours, days, months, and years. He escaped into fantasies. As a child, he would fantasize about people obeying him while he was at the center of attention. In particular, he fantasized about situations in which he had full control, a sense of power reassuring him that he was no longer alone and helpless. These fantasies began to come true when he was in high school. At first sporadically and hesitantly, and later assertively and consistently, Jim Jones would put on a cloak, stand in the street, and preach to the people, especially to the homeless, blacks, unemployed, and drunks, who were ready to listen to him and respond. Reading his success in the yearning eyes of his listeners, he made this a regular practice. The young Jim began traveling to neighboring towns, hitching rides in cars and on public transport. He soon found the streets where the destitute and wretched gathered, and there he would stand at the street corners and preach to the people, who drank in his words thirstily.

Like many of the great charismatic types, he had tremendous ability to express emotions. As one of his believers described it: "He listened like nobody else could, his black eyes glowing with empathy and love."[14] Jim Jones made people feel like they had never felt before. He revealed such empathy for their suffering and desires that even those who left his temple spoke of his great ability to understand their feelings, emotions, and thoughts.

Jones modeled his behavior on the black leader from Harlem, Father Devine. Jones learned from him how to conduct public confessions and ruthless public interrogations. He recruited unswerving commitment through these public confessions and through the publicity given to the cult members' declarations and promises at these meetings.

His behavior (in contrast to his inner feeling) was markedly unambivalent. He was determined, unequivocal, and uncompromising in confronting his followers over their commitments. The effect of his determination and "knowing the right way" was heightened by the distance he kept from his believers. He did not deal with the everyday details of organizing the community; he did not handle technical aspects or "hang out" with his people. His external behavior was far removed from his inner world. He spoke of another, better world, more just, more beautiful. He spoke of love, but his inner world was melancholy, and death was often in his thoughts. Years later, when he was interviewed in jail, he said that in his heart he had been dead for a long time, and it was only his desire to help others who depended on him that kept him going. He said to his interviewers:

Ever since as a child I saw a dog die, I wanted to commit suicide. It was the first time I felt guilt. But I still had some little dogs and cats alive, and I had to keep care of them, so I stayed alive for some thirty-nine years more. . . . Then a little later, my mom needed me, and then some poor soul down the road, poor and minority. Then always blacks wanted me for their champion. It's always been that way.[15]

To Jones, the meaning of life was uncertainty, betrayal, alienation, rejection, and loneliness. All these were relieved temporarily and partially by people's dependence on him and by the omnipotence that was built around this dependence. But deep inside himself, he knew that this was a temporary refuge, and death was the final escape. Jones liked the idea of death. When we look at his life, sick and drugged, constantly struggling for grandeur, we reach the conclusion that cracks in the structure of the dependence and the omnipotence he created led inevitably to the growth of his death wish. The temporary refuge was not an adequate protection.

And that is what happened in the end. The Jones cult's activities came under the scrutiny of the American Congress, which instigated an inquiry. The cult members moved to Guiana and set up camp there (Jonestown, of course) in the woods. At a certain stage, the inquiry commission, headed by Congressman William Ryan, arrived in Jonestown. Then Jones felt that his paranoid vision was reaching fruition. At first he tried to restrain himself and even welcomed the Congress delegation with a show of hospitality, but he soon reached a breaking point. It happened when some members of the cult asked to leave Jonestown and return to the United States with the Congress delegation. Jones saw this as undermining the solid and uniform world of the cult; everything was collapsing and being destroyed by the forces of Satan. From then on, Jones prepared the death scene. He told his believers that there were CIA agents in the jungle; he initiated abortive attacks, and thus, in the terror-stricken, paranoid situation that developed, suicide was presented as a "revolutionary victory," escape from a cruel and corrupt world, and entrance into history. But, more important, this was the ultimate and absolute triumph of the power of Jones's love, love that would finally unite his followers with him, in unity with death, which Jones described so typically as "the orgasm of the grave." To Jones, his followers' fate was not a matter of concern. They were merely projections of himself: miserable and weak people, whom he could not leave behind on his journey to death. "I did not bring you this far only to leave you with no future, with nobody to love you, to plan for you and take care of you."[16]

And thus death gradually began to lose its threatening meaning in the eyes of the cult members. Like their leader, they began to internalize the belief that they were surrounded by a hostile world. They were ready to share the ultimate emptiness with the man who would take them with him to eternity. It was not Jim Jones who had driven them to this extreme step, but the outside world. They perceived Jones as the antithesis of that world. This was aptly expressed by Ann Moore in her last letter before the suicide: "Jim was the most honest, loving and considerate person I have ever met. He knew how cruel the world is. His love for people is indescribable. Jim Jones showed us that we can live with differences, and we are all human beings. We are going to die because we are not allowed to live in peace."[17]

ADOLF HITLER

A famous researcher on leadership lectured at an important seminar in the United States. The subject of the lecture was leadership. At the end of the lecture, he was asked who he thought was the greatest leader of the twentieth century. To his listeners' astonishment, he replied: "Hitler," adding, "the reason is that Adolf Hitler influenced the largest number of people. Millions followed him, were ready to die for him, were ready to kill for him."

Hitler influenced millions of people, poor and ignorant as well as industrialists, manufacturers, bankers, and intellectuals. The range of his influence and its extreme manifestations have focused the attention of historians, psychologists, and sociologists on the Hitler phenomenon to an unparalleled degree.

The key to understanding Hitler's personality probably lies in three factors: his physical constitution, his parents, and perhaps also the side effects of meningitis.[18] Physically, he was quite meager and feeble and lacked one testicle. His father, a cold and authoritarian figure, was often away from home, and his mother was overpermissive and overprotective.

Even without the side effects of meningitis, this collection of factors did not bode well for his future personality. When he left home, he settled in Vienna and tried to be an artist. In fact, he lived in poverty in third-rate hostels. He was not accepted to study at the Vienna Academy of Art, which hurt him. He kept away from people and lived a wretched existence. Apparently he was also sexually deviant. According to the evidence of his friends, he was very near to having a mental breakdown. He was a paranoiac, hostile, suspicious, and riddled with feelings of shame. His biographers write that these feelings of shame were deep and constant. He was ashamed of his failure at school (he gave expression to it by using the document expelling him from school as toilet paper) and of his repeated failures to be admitted to the academy. He was ashamed of descending to the level of the Viennese rabble when he was forced to sell "artistic products," which he himself regarded with contempt.[19]

Hitler was also ashamed of his physical defects and his sexual deviations. He lived in chronic anxiety of embarrassing himself; of looking ridiculous; seeming inferior, weak, or unfit; or of being defeated or humiliated (he never agreed to have a complete physical checkup).[20]

Hitler was constantly motivated by the basic fear of losing his supporters, who were, after all, the main confirmation of his worth; this pattern persisted when he was in a position of leadership. He demanded loyalty, admiration, and submission from those around him. As with Jim Jones and Charles Manson, there were extreme contradictions in his personality. On the one hand, he could behave gently with children, and on the other hand, he was capable of loathsome cruelty, enjoying the sight of torture, particularly when it was connected with some hurt to himself and his self-esteem. For example, he ordered the use of a piano string for the slow strangulation of those who plotted against him (Von Stauffenberg and the group of officers who made an abortive attempt on his life on July 20, 1944).

According to many who have written about his personality, Hitler had a typical borderline personality, characterized by sharp contradictions and paranoid splitting. On the one hand, self-grandiosity, and on the other hand, a deep feeling of inner emptiness. This hypothesis is supported by behavioral evidence. Borderline types stand out in their ability to fill various roles with great conviction while maintaining a distance and to identify emotional nuances in others and exploit them.

As with Jones and Manson, the theme of death is clearly evident. The closeness to death, the fascination with death, are not accidental. Hitler always claimed that he did not have a long time to live, and he was motivated by the sense that death was lying in wait for him. Moreover, his emergence as a leader was born out of the closeness to death. According to the evidence of his feelings, he was really born again during his military service in World War I, where he excelled as a platoon commander. The state of war was an elixir of life for him, as he himself described it: "War is life, war is the origin of all things, any struggle is war."[21]

ANALYSIS OF THE LEADERSHIP PHENOMENON

The Great Compensation

What are the sources of this desire to be at center stage, to be admired and adored, to have influence and power? This desire, this need, is so overpowering in certain people that it seems to be the only thing that gives meaning to their life. It seems as if the position of leadership offers the only salvation and without it, death, which is forever knocking on the door, is the only alternative.

The biographies of Jim Jones, Charles Manson, and Adolf Hitler (and other leaders who will be mentioned later) may perhaps provide answers to this question. A reading of these biographies reveals certain manifestations that seem to reflect a pattern beyond mere coincidence. Some scholars have referred to this pattern, but it has yet to be comprehensively discussed. This I will attempt to do here.

The first and simplest explanation of this pattern is lack of love. There is a great deal of research evidence of the effect of this lack on various obsessions. In a well-known experiment conducted by Harlow[22] it was found that monkey pups preferred an artificial mother-substitute made of soft cloth to a surrogate made of wire but equipped with a milk-dispensing nipple. Apparently, the soft touch of terry cloth is more soothing than milk. If animals feel loved by their parents, the true source of these feelings may lie in the experience of warmth and softness. There is no doubt that human beings begin to feel loved in response to signs of affection including touching, hugging, and stroking. Other experiments by Harlow[23] showed that monkey pups that were separated from their mothers suffered psychological or physical disability throughout their lives. Various studies have shown clearly that the absence of parents, even for short periods, is apt to have negative effects. For children placed in orphanages and similar institutions, the damage is liable to be permanent.[24]

Wolff, in his book *Children under Stress*, found a correlation between the loss of parents in childhood and various psychiatric and social disturbances in adulthood. Personality disturbances, neuro-

ses, delinquency, and suicide attempts among adults are all statistically related to the experience of unstable family life.[25] A study
comparing various groups of children found that, in a group that
regularly visited psychiatric clinics, the number of children who
had lost their parents was double the number of children with parents and of children who regularly visited dental clinics.[26]

One could cite dozens of findings of this type, but the principle is
clear: The feeling of lack of love, in the simplest sense of absence of
affection, becomes a driving force. This force takes various expressions: the desire to be famous and loved, the wish to be compensated orally and sexually (for example, overeating is often related
to the absence of breast feeding in infancy, or the search for warmth
through sex); briefly, the feeling of lack of affection drives the individual to seek compensatory solutions.[27] The need to be a leader, to
be at the center, to be loved are among the possible compensations
for this feeling, which is often unconscious. This mechanism is not
necessarily related only to leadership; it may find expression in
many forms. The idea of compensation was discussed by Freud
and, more emphatically, by one of his most famous students, Alfred
Adler. It is not surprising that these two saw compensation as a central psychological process. They were both medical doctors and
their way of thinking was based on biological observation, which
became psychobiological (with Freud). They discerned that the biological organism is capable of initiating compensatory processes.
Thus, when a person loses the sight of one eye, the other eye becomes functionally stronger to compensate for the blinded one. The
same process operates in the case of hearing loss, injury to the
limbs, and so forth: Various organs in the body find a way to compensate for lack of other parts by improved functioning. This principle applies also to psychological processes. For example, Adler
spoke of inferiority complex as a typical cause of a compensatory
dynamic. Somewhat simplified, it goes as follows: An academically
weak student attempts to excel at a sport. Leadership, according to
this explanation, is a possible type of compensation.

A salient example of analysis of a leader based on the "compensation argument" is George and George's well-known book on

Woodrow Wilson, who was president of the United States during World War I.[28] Their study, the first of its kind, showed clearly how the acts of a leader are influenced by his personality. The book centered on what was defined as "the concept of compensatory character formation." The argument is that "power acts to restore the self-esteem that was severely damaged in childhood" (p. 320). The authors explain very convincingly that Wilson was guided unequivocally by the powerful urge to overcome the feeling of inferiority that his father had worked hard to instill in him by humiliating him, mocking him, making the child Wilson the butt of the cynical wit and sarcasm that was inherent in the father's bitter nature. Accumulating strength and using it in politics became Wilson's way "to conquer and exorcise the demons of his childhood" (p. 320).

Another type of explanation that can be seen as an extension, a deepening, and a refinement of the previous argument (and may also lead to more specific predictions) is the narcissistic explanation, which centers around the phenomenon of mirroring. The word "mirror" comes from the Latin root *mirari*, meaning not just "to look at" but also to admire. *Mirari* is also connected with the word "mirage"—optical illusion. A mirror is therefore a possible tool both for seeing a true reflection and for distorting it. A mirror can be a screen on which images are projected. Indeed, this theme is prevalent, in many variations, in legends, folklore stories, and myths. The most famous myth about the mirroring effect is, of course, Ovid's story of Narcissus, a beautiful youth who saw his reflection in a pool of water, fell in love with it, and could not tear his eyes away from it until he died of exhaustion—he loved himself to death.

The term "narcissism" has become a major psychodynamic concept. In fact, as Pines[29] points out, "Narcissism is a paradigm of the role of mirroring in the development of self awareness" (p. 33). Through mirroring, the individual creates projections, overcomes inhibitions, and forms his ideas and images. The mirror metaphor implies a possible multiplication of images, which can, of course, lead to severance (sometimes fatal, as history shows) of the private awareness from the public awareness. What we want to see and what we fear to see may be totally different worlds. As psychohistorical works indicate, there are people who do not succeed in harmonizing the images. History contains some outstanding examples of such people, who sometimes became extremely destructive.[30] Ferenczi, one of Freud's students, said that the moment of looking in the mirror is the moment of truth between all-powerful narcissistic forces and reality.[31]

The first sense of self, the moment when the individual begins to relate to himself as an entity, starts with seeing his reflection in the mirror. Winnicott[32] claims that this formative experience of self-identification begins with the baby's reflection in his mother's eyes, his mother's face. "What the baby sees is himself or herself. In other words, the mother is looking at the baby and what she looks like is related to what she sees there" (p. 112).

According to Winnicott, the baby's reflection in his mother's face (and later in the mirror) and his sensitivity to changes he perceives in these reflections are of considerable significance in his emotional development. (This process explains why we continue to see in others part of ourselves, our fears, our failures, and our yearnings.) The conventional psychological assumption is that a healthy process of maturation is expressed in the degree of realism that exists in these reflections. The nature and quality of the mirroring relationship with the mother will strongly affect the individual's ability for realistic examination of the world around him. As Romanyshyn writes,[33] "Mirroring is a primary and central phenomenon in human life. It begins before the end of the first year and does not disappear even after the rational elements appear in the adult's awareness" (p. 64).

Heinz Kohut[34] gave a boost to the concept of mirroring, both at the conceptual level and in applying the concept as a therapeutic term in clinical practice. Kohut saw mirroring as a normal stage in the development of the infant. This stage of development is characterized by what Kohut defines as the "grandiose self." "The child attempts to save the originally all-embracing narcissism by concentrating perfection and power in the self . . . and by turning away disdainfully from an outside to which all imperfections have been assigned" (p. 160).

Like Winnicott, Kohut emphasizes the importance of the mother's face as a mirror, the mother whose shining eyes demonstrate her adoration of her child, the lovable and perfect baby, who receives all his narcissistic and exhibitionist needs through the mother's constant adoration. The grandiose self is thus a necessary and even healthy stage in the child's development (in the early stages, of course). Lichtenstein[35] claims that the formation of the primary identity is always based on the experience of mirroring. The mirror is what creates the primary identity, but later, the pure total reflection has to be gradually replaced by more selective processes.

Pines[36] distinguishes between what he defines as reflective and nonreflective mirroring. In reflective mirroring, the person accepts his good and bad qualities, while in nonreflective mirroring there is distortion of the ego and selective perception of the self.

We can sum up and say that the mirroring process is a central, though manipulative, part of identity formation. It can sometimes be seen as a theater, and it is hard to distinguish between the actor and the audience. It is a process by which a person may lose or find his identity. Furthermore, the way in which an individual manages this process expresses the degree of his maturity, but there is no doubt that distortion of the reflection endangers realistic self-perception.

I have dwelt on this explanation of narcissism and mirroring because these processes form the basis for another explanation for the emergence of outstanding leaders and their resolute behavior. Basically, leadership may be connected with narcissism and mirroring in two ways: The first is damage to the mirroring process, in the sense of "deprivation" during the process of building the grandiose self, deprivation of the amount of narcissism that is necessary for all development. This deprivation may stem from the absence of a loving and adoring mother, either in the actual physical sense (such as orphanhood), or in the sense of a stable maternal relationship. In these circumstances, the child is likely to grow up with a strong desire to compensate for the deprivation, to seek the missing adoration, striving to be the grandiose self in later stages of life, when this wish is no longer relevant and true testing of reality is appropriate.

The other possible connection with leadership is the full, perhaps exaggerated, existence of the mirroring processes that create the grandiose self. The baby is adored completely. The damage does not lie here, but in the inability to separate from these processes, as normal development requires. The difficulty lies in creating self distinction, a separate and autonomous identity, formed by gradual distancing from the symbiotic relationship with the mother, a process known in the professional literature as separation and individuation.[37] This stage is characterized by the presence of two parallel processes: separation—leading to separate awareness, and "individuation"—leading to an inner sense of autonomy. A substage of this is rapprochement, characterized by the child's making slight attempts to separate himself from the symbiotic relationship with the mother. For example, he moves away from her a little and then runs back to touch her and so on, back and forth. The child seeks to assure himself that his mother does not disappear when he moves away from her. As the perception of "permanence of the object" (the mother) becomes more firmly established, the child is capable of moving away from her without fear of being abandoned or fear that the object will disappear. Successful transition through the stage of separation and individuation leads to the formation of the sense of self, of being a physical and mental entity with a clearly defined body and ego and a feeling of autonomy.

Winnicott sees the ability to be alone as one of the important expressions of emotional maturity. In describing normal development, Winnicott speaks of development from absolute dependence to relative independence, from lack of distinction between the self and the object to the development of distinct selfhood and autonomy.

To describe a mother who treats her child intuitively and adequately, Winnicott coined the phrase "good enough mother," a mother whose response is compatible with development, and this compatibility is what permits normal development. For our purposes, damage at the stage of separation and individuation leaves the child in the stage of the grandiose self, and that is how he will stay—yearning for this kind of feeling, this kind of grandiosity. In both cases, deprivation or incomplete separation and individuation, the prediction is for the same result: the striving to be great, strong, adored—to be grandiose. Both these sources of motivation lead in the same direction.

Another explanation for the insatiable yearning, the obsessive desire to be a leader, is associated mainly with Abraham Zaleznik, an eminent professor at the Harvard School of Business Management.[38] Zaleznik, who provided psychoanalytical consultation to managers (and taught a course called Psychoanalysis and Leadership at Harvard), sees the powerful urge to be a leader as a wish "to be born again." Zaleznik argues that the biographies of many leaders of the "obsessive type" are characterized by the absence of a father, either in the actual physical sense (death, divorce, abandonment), or in the psychological sense of being estranged, distant, drunk, cruel; in other words, a father "who was not there for the child." In every case, the child's basic experience is one of constant anxiety resulting from a deep sense of lack of control and uncertainty as to what lies in store. This experience creates a strong desire to control the surroundings. Thus, according to the explanations of Zaleznik and others, leadership becomes an inner experience of what Zaleznik defines as "twice born." The helpless child, lacking a strong father to lean on, becomes his own corrected father, a strong father. And in fact, characteristics that support this line of thinking may be found in several outstanding psychobiographical analyses.[39]

Hitler's father was a rigid and stern bureaucrat, twenty-three years older than his wife. When at home, the father underwent a metamorphosis: He became a tyrant who beat his wife and children. Hitler was afraid of his father, he feared his sudden outbursts, and the more he feared the more dependent he became on his mother's love and affection, which obstructed the process of separation and individuation. Hitler's speaking of Germany as the motherland rather than the more common expression, fatherland, was apparently not fortuitous. Also, his attitude toward the Jews as the rapists of Germany appears to be connected with his constant inner experience.

The example of Hitler's family is extreme, but the personal stories of other outstanding leaders also contain elements of alienation and fear of the father, even when they do not reveal the degree of brutality that marks Hitler's father and their family dynamics seem normal to the casual viewer. A deeper scrutiny indicates the same pattern that motivates the later wish to gain control over the threatening uncertainty.

Gandhi, for example, was born into an upper middle-class family. His father was the governor of Porbandar province. He married Gandhi's mother (his fourth wife) when he was more than forty years old and twice her age; Gandhi was the last child of a young woman and an aging patriarch. His attitude to his father was ambivalent: He both admired and feared him. His father was always busy, distant, did not devote time to him, and never related to him intimately. On the other hand, he had a close and loving relationship with his young mother.

Other scholars have seen in these examples a different or expanded pattern of the twice born explanation. For example, Burns[40] characterizes these examples as a state of unresolved conflict: loving one side and hating the other. This state of intimate love for the mother and hatred of the father is a kind of magnified oedipal conflict, which is normally resolved by accepting the father's authority, according to Freud. But in these situations, there is no father whose authority can be accepted, and the psychological element necessary for solution of the oedipal conflict is missing. This increases the urge to be one's own father and resolve the unbearable oedipal conflict in this way. (Indeed, some examples found in children's literature show that the children saw themselves as fathers to their mothers.)

In the manner of academic typologies, the explanations offered here are schematic in the sense that they demand the formulation of categories. In reality, no explanation completely matches a given category. The examples cited here indicate this clearly. For example, Hitler could have been motivated by the need to conquer uncertainty (twice born), but his close relations with his mother could equally explain both his possible fixation at the stage of the grandiose self (according to Kohut and Winnicott), or alternatively (or in addition), an intense oedipal conflict seeking a solution through becoming a strong father and a strong leader. Similarly, Gandhi and many leaders like him reveal all the elements of the various categories of explanation. There are other cases where certain explanations can be applied more distinctly (for example, the case of Manson). One way or another, according to these explanations, the powerful yearning to be a leader, to be accepted as a leader, to behave as a leader, has its sources in a specific early childhood and is a kind of "great compensation," a genuine psychological rescue. The emotional significance of this is sometimes immensely vital and is powerfully transmitted to the followers.

Let us now consider the emotional effect of such leaders.

The Emotional Link

A few years ago, a French film was released that dealt with the nuances of relationships between men and women, particularly the initial surprising and sometimes incomprehensible attraction between them. The film starts with an original scene: a woman striding along. We see only her shapely legs, sheathed in nylon stockings, emerging from a black skirt or dress. The viewer's eyes follow the legs striding along the paths of a cemetery (we do not see her face or body), passing graves and finally stopping beside the shapely legs of another woman, who is standing next to an open grave. The scene is repeated several times: the high-heeled legs of another woman marching to the same grave, until half a dozen pairs of pretty legs stand around the grave. Then the camera slowly ascends the women's bodies and comes to rest on their faces, focusing on the tearful eyes while the coffin is lowered into the grave and covered by mounds of earth.

In the next scene, all these women are sitting around a table in a nearby café and talking about the dead man. It appears that he was their lover and beloved. The question the women wonder about is what was the secret of his charm? More precisely, how did he succeed in making them want to be with him, to respond to his wooing? They all agree that he was not particularly good-looking. "He was so short," says one. Another adds, "He was so fragile." The women search for an answer to the riddle that puzzles them. Finally one of them says, "He wanted so much! He radiated such passion, such desire, that it was impossible to withstand." Murmurs of agreement confirm that the other women share this feeling. The strong sexual desire was expressed most powerfully, but above all it was received as such beyond the usual feelings and messages. There was no objective explanation for this powerful effect, but they all felt it. This example of the power of desire serves as an analogy of the desire for power at its most intensive level. This is how people like Jim Jones, Charles Manson, and Adolf Hitler, in their boundless yearning to be at the center of people's interest, to influence them, to arouse their admiration, expressed this desire so openly and bluntly that the vitality it acquired overshadowed the limitations of their outward appearance. They were able to transmit emotions in a way that deeply touched the people who heard and saw them.

One of the members of the "family" described how Manson held talks in which he gave strong expression to his hatred for the outside world, along with protection, love, desire, and sexuality toward "his family"—his believers.[41]

Hitler's ability to appeal to emotions is described in similar terms: "Hitler's ability to shift from one mood to another was amazing. One moment his eyes were full of tears and deep affection, a moment later his mood changed to anger with flashing eyes, and this gave way at once to a glazed look, as if he were watching a vision being formed."[42]

Thus it seems that leaders of this kind have an ability that is not merely histrionic. There is much more here than acting ability. The common factor that emerges from analysis of observations and evidence presented by researchers on these leaders is the unequivocal feeling that this is not acting but authentic expression. It seems, as described by Dixon, that this behavior is "like war." "Such leaders were constantly motivated [to influence] by the basic fear of losing their supporters, who were the main confirmation of their being people of value."[43]

Winston Churchill expressed this urge most aptly in describing himself and those like him: "Famous men are usually the product of unhappy childhood. The stern compression of circumstances, the twinge of adversity, the spur of slights and taunts in early years are needed to evoke that ruthless fixity of purpose and tenacious mother wit without which great actions are seldom accomplished."[44]

These descriptions and arguments can hardly be applied to all leaders (I will return to this point later); I refer at the moment to extreme cases when the urge to lead was obsessive. It is not easy to explain the nature of that uncontrolled obsessive urge. It is an urge so strong, so extreme, unconscious and irrational that it is hard for most people to conceive of its existence, let alone understand it. Unlike affection, love, hate, and friendship, known and familiar emotions that arouse personal associations, the obsessive urge—and certainly the obsessive urge described here—is missing in the repertoire of experiences of most people. To demonstrate the nature of an uncontrolled obsessive urge, I will cite a case that was publicized in Meyer Levin's famous novel, *Obsession*, which describes graphically the immense unconscious force of the obsession. The novel tells the story of a murder committed by two young men from good families, and the case is analyzed brilliantly in a book by Israel Or-Bach.[45]

The author starts by describing the background of the young men, Judd Steiner and Artie Strauss. Judd, who was orphaned as a young boy, suffered from an ongoing trauma during his childhood. His birth was a big disappointment to his mother, who wanted a girl. She tried to "correct" nature's "mistake" and treated Judd as a girl, dressed him as a girl, and even sent him to a girls' school. At the same time, he had a caregiver who taught him the secrets of sex through practical experience. As a result, Judd was confused regarding his personal and sexual identity, and traumatized by his early exposure to sexual relations. His mother's death was an added blow. In contrast, Artie is described as a person with a profound, unconquerable hatred that stemmed from feeling rejected and unloved by his family. His hatred, combined with the admiration he received from those around him, crystallized into a belief that he was unique, exceptional, and essentially different from other mortals. Judd hero-worshipped Artie and became dependent on him. They developed a homosexual relationship, which compensated Judd for the trauma of premature sexual experience and his stolen masculine identity. The two partners in crime enticed a neighbor's son into their car and strangled him to death. They parked for a while by the cemetery, then drove to a place they had chosen in advance, and there they stripped their victim, poured acid on his face and sex organs in order to blur his identity, and buried him in the opening of a pipe in a culvert, surrounded by bushes that drained sewage and water into a swamp. Afterward, they sent extortion letters to the boy's parents, claiming that he was alive and demanding 10,000 dollars for his release.

In fact, the perfect crime turned out to be no more than a series of stupid mistakes. Judd left his reading glasses beside the child's body. These glasses led directly to him because they were a special prescription. The extortion attempt failed at an early stage. The hiding place of the body was not good because the bridge over the culvert was used by many people. What is more, they did not push the body deep into the pipe. If they had pushed it a few centimeters further in, the body would not have been found. In the book, Dr. Weiss, the psychoanalyst, discusses the sources of the two murderers' behavior. Judd's father wanted boys to be boys and behave like boys, to be unruly and boisterous, but his mother was obsessive about cleanliness and tidiness. Judd had these characteristics. He was compulsively tidy, and his confusion about whether he was a boy or girl became worse and worse. As Dr. Weiss remarks, we should also remember Judd's painful experience at the girls' school he attended. He was not allowed to enter the school lavatory and he had to control his bladder. These experiences affected his masculinity, his sexual tendencies, and his sexual identity. Judd's trouble was that his sexual insecurity never left him. He did not know whether he was a boy or a girl. He struggled with himself constantly, fighting to be a male. And thus the explanation ramifies, the connecting thread being the claim that nothing is "accidental" in the end. The boy's murder, according to this explanation, was an attempt to resolve Judd's terrible inner conflict concerning his sexual identity. The boy's murder was destruction of the male element in himself. Judd wanted to destroy the male element and return his body to the womb. But can we, perhaps, see his actions as a wish to correct a mistake, because he felt that he should have been born a girl? In Dr. Weiss's view, Judd did not plan a crime but an obsessive repetition of the initial childhood trauma, a kind of continuation of "correcting nature," which his mother had started. The same applies to Artie. One of the psychoanalyst's hypotheses is that Artie wanted to murder his younger brother, who was the same age as the victim and had "stolen" his parents' love.

Uncontrolled obsession is a major characteristic of the unconscious mind. The psychoanalytic approach sees behavior as being forced on the individual in spite of his wishes and without his knowledge. According to this explanation, both Artie and Judd were the captives of strong but invisible forces, and their compulsive behavior was motivated by an unconscious wish, sexual in Judd's case and aggressive in Artie's.

This example illustrates the possible weight of unconscious compulsive forces. Psychoanalysts tend to assume that, in hypnotic leaders, the subconscious creates a dynamic of destruction. This is an ungovernable need. An eminent French psychiatrist, Maurice Choisy, spoke explicitly of this and even called it the Phaeton complex, after Phaeton, the son of Phoebus, the sun god in Greek mythology.[46] Two things worried young Phaeton: Did his father really love him, and was he, Phaeton, illegitimate? When these two questions were put to Phoebus, he was so shocked that he did not merely declare his love for Phaeton but swore to fulfill his every request. Phaeton quickly took advantage of this rash promise and asked to drive the sun chariot. The father, who knew his son's limitations, was not eager, but he had promised, so he reluctantly handed the reins to his son. It soon became clear that the father's doubts were justified, Phaeton was not equal to the task. Fortunately, the sun's strange behavior in crossing the sky was noticed by Zeus, the king of the gods. Worried that a terrible fire would break out if the sun touched the earth, Zeus shot a lightning bolt at Phaeton, who fell and sank into a river. His charred body was taken from the river and buried by diligent water nymphs.

Choisy describes the Phaeton complex as a painful combination of thoughts and emotions caused by the parent's lack of love, due to their absence, loss, coldness, or traumatic experiences caused by them. The result is frustration, leading to aggressiveness. Rejected love turns into hatred. The great danger of the Phaeton complex, according to Choisy, is that the person suffering from it is not aware of the complex (if he were, he might be able to overcome it). According to the inner logic of the unconscious, he is not aware because the events that caused the complex were so painful that he prefers to forget them. This suppression of the memory has two harmful results: The individual's behavior is destructive to himself as well as to others because he is not aware of the motives behind the behavior and society completely ignores the Phaeton complex because it is denied by the self and effectively hidden from the eyes of others.

The British psychologist Norman Dixon attained great publicity with this argument. He published two books on famous leaders in history whose characters and actions were marked by the common factors of hypnotic influence and destructiveness. One book was on military leaders[47] and the other was on mainly political leaders. The name of the second book testifies clearly to the central idea presented in it in dozens of variations: *Our Own Worst Enemy: The Psychology of Unsuccessful Leaderships*.[48]

Good and Bad Charismatic Leaders

Even if we stay in the realm of theory and psychoanalytic explanations, the question still remains to be asked: Does an unhappy childhood always lead to the same type of obsessive urge that produces Hitlers, Joneses, Mansons, and other hypnotic or destructive figures? This formula appears oversimplistic and one-dimensional. Mahatma Gandhi, David Ben Gurion, Charles de Gaulle, Winston Churchill, and many others were also charismatic leaders, and even if we can identify unhappy dynamics in their childhoods, as Churchill said about himself, their contribution was in most cases far from destructive. On the contrary, it was positive by every accepted criterion. In no way are they identified with destruction and death, as are Hitler, Jones, and Manson. Statistically, too, the number of destructive hypnotic leaders is smaller than the number of nondestructive ones, so if we want to understand the full range of "psychodynamic correction" that underlies the urge to be a leader, we need to seek other explanations that can predict the development of both destructive tendencies and positive directions in leadership. Exceptionally charismatic leaders appear at both extremes.

I have referred here to three explanations for what I defined as "correction," which underlies the powerful wish to be famous or to be a leader.

One explanation is what Zaleznik[49] calls twice born. As described earlier, Zaleznik argues that the urge to be a leader is the urge to rid oneself of anxiety and uncertainty due to the absence (physical or psychological) of a father figure. The position of leadership gives the individual control of the situation. The leader has an inner experience that motivates him, in Zaleznik's words, to be his own corrected father. Zaleznik's argument is supported by evidence that can hardly be seen as incidental. For example, Lucille Iremonger, a British scholar, while gathering material for a biography of twenty-four British prime ministers, from Spencer Percival in 1809 to Neville Chamberlain in 1937, was surprised to discover that fifteen of them, that is, sixty-six percent, had lost a father in childhood. Examining the population census for 1921, Iremonger found that only about two percent of the general population had been orphaned in childhood.[50]

The second explanation is lack of sufficient warmth and love, as described in a character analysis of Woodrow Wilson.[51] The argument is that the position of leadership enables these emotionally deprived individuals to gain the love, interest, and attention of people—things that they lack and long for.

The third explanation refers to narcissistic deprivation, damage done during the process of adoration for the baby. This distinguishes between someone who becomes a good leader and one who becomes destructive. I expand on this explanation because it is the one most relevant to the subjects at the core of this discussion: the pathological aspects in the phenomenon of leadership, which are manifested in extreme cases with extreme examples.

Researcher Jane Howell made an important contribution in distinguishing between "socialized charismatic leaders," who are positive and good leaders, and "personalized charismatic leaders," who are negative and destructive.[52] This distinction is of considerable value in the attempt to develop methodologies for classification of leaders. However, there has been little research on developmental processes of leaders, certainly not at the rate of developmental psychology in general.

To clarify the importance of the narcissistic argument in explaining the distinction between socialized and personalized charismatic leaders, we need to elaborate on the discussion of narcissism beyond the explanation given above.

According to Kohut,[53] the normal development of the self involves both narcissistic development and development of love for an object (derived from mirroring) during infancy. The grandiosity fantasy, far from being pathological in essence, is vital to development. It becomes pathological only when its development is disturbed. According to this approach, a narcissistic disturbance occurs when the narcissistic self does not receive sufficient support for its development. Kohut describes the etiology of narcissistic disturbance as deriving from "deprivation," deprivation of support for the narcissistic self, particularly because of the parents' failure to give their child enough adoration. In the absence of such support, two processes may occur, which result finally in personality disturbance. The first is that the grandiosity fantasy is severely damaged, leaving the individual wounded and insecure. The second is that the lack of support in the development of the narcissistic self causes the individual to turn to idealization of himself. In other words, insufficient adoration from the parents forces the child to provide his own adoration. This effort requires great energy and sometimes comes at the expense of emotional investment in others.

The developmental argument states that in the transition to adulthood, the child has to process the grandiosity fantasy gradually with the support of those close to him. In his relationships with these people, two types of transference occur: delaying transference and mirroring transference. In both types, the child forms the image of an ideal object, in which he sees himself reflected as in a mirror. In this way, his self-image receives the support necessary for its development, and the grandiosity fantasy develops. However, herein lies the danger. The grandiosity fantasy causes the subject to see reality as he wants to see it, while normal development means constant improvement of his ability to examine reality. There are milestones in the modification of the grandiosity fantasy: recognition of other people as individuals in their own right with their good and bad qualities and recognition of one's personal limitations and the limitations of reality required for the creation of a value system. All these are part of normal development. Narcissistic disturbance is reflected in the personality by self-absorption compounded with vulnerability and self-adoration. The formal diagnosis defines a person with narcissistic disturbances as follows:

1. Has a sense of grandiosity and self-importance (exaggerates his achievements and talents, expects to be recognized as superior without proving it by achievements);
2. Fantasizes about great success, brilliance, beauty, or ideal love;
3. Believes he is special and can only be understood by special people or those with high status or connected with God;
4. Demands constant admiration;
5. Feels that things are his due, has unrealistic expectations of receiving privileges or gaining automatic acceptance of all his expectations;
6. Is exploitative, ignores the rights of others, exploits others for his needs;
7. Lacks empathy, does not want to see the needs of others or recognize them;
8. Often envies others and believes that they envy him;
9. Is subject to strong feelings of anger or shame, humiliation, and emptiness (DSM, p. 661).[54]

We should note that we are discussing a phenomenon that has various levels of intensity. Freud himself[55] argues that intensive self-love is formative in childhood, and he calls it "primary narcissism." Later, this narcissism develops into the subject's relation to others, for example, a parent's investment in his children; he devotes himself to them as if they were part of himself and sometimes even tries to "make improvements" in them, to spare them his suffering, to give them what he missed, and so forth. Following emotional damage, says Freud, a person is liable to find himself in a pathological state defined by Freud as "secondary narcissism."

Kernberg,[56] too, who studied narcissism in depth, distinguishes between levels of severity in the narcissistic disturbance. The first level is characterized by regression from normal narcissism to primary narcissism. In this condition, most of the person's qualities are retained. The second level is characterized by disturbance in object relations, when the people around him become extensions of his own personality and he selects certain identifications and devalues others. The third, most severe level is very problematic in terms of human relations. In this condition there are no longer object relations in the usual sense, but relations between a grandiose self and its projections on others.

Leaders driven by a narcissistic urge differ in their inner feelings from other leaders. The sources of this drive are specific: They seek admiration, they do not seek human contacts. This is reflected in their sense of boundless loneliness, as described so clearly by Jones, Hitler, and Manson themselves. But this is not loneliness in the usual sense of the word. When we speak of loneliness in everyday life, we usually refer to an individual's feelings in a certain social context or relationship. However, studies conducted on loneliness show that the feeling of loneliness itself is not necessarily connected with present experiences or interactions. A person can have a deep sense of loneliness, of being alone, regardless of external circumstances, even when he is with people who love him. This loneliness stems from the longing for an integrated inner condition.[57] Thus, loneliness is not a specific uniform experience but, as pointed out by two researchers in this field, there are several types of loneliness. The first type reflects social alienation, experienced mainly in situations when the individual lacks social contacts. The second type, paranoid loneliness, includes feelings of anger toward others, a sense that others do not understand. This type is connected mainly with lack of intimate contacts, situations of loss, or separation from a loved one. The third type, depressive loneliness, includes feelings of depression combined with longing for a loved one. This type, too, is associated with lack of intimate relationships. The fourth type of loneliness, relevant to this discussion of personalized charismatic leaders, is defined in the literature as narcissistic loneliness. This type of loneliness is not related to outside circumstances. As one of the researchers writes, this loneliness "reflects intrapsychic conflicts related to the formation of self identity" (p. 92).[58] This loneliness, as described by the psychoanalyst Fromm-Reichman, has its source in early experiences, in early relationships at the preverbal stage, when the basic sense of loneliness was stamped on the individual's personality and later was to become an insatiable hunger for admiration.

The important points in this argument relate mainly to the extreme pathological levels of narcissistic disturbance. What is important here is the combination of tireless fostering of the grandiose self and utter indifference and lack of interest in others. This, in my view, is the combination that underlies the pattern of personalized charismatic leadership. In the other two forms of "correction," the subject is not indifferent to those around him. On the contrary, he longs for love or strives relentlessly for control, perhaps struggling to be loved by others as a compensation. This is what the socialized charismatic leader does. He is eager for the love of others, he sees himself through them and them through himself; they are very important to him because they are the source of love, approval, or feelings of control.

In the case of narcissistic disturbance, the individual does not struggle for love in the sense of warmth (as in Harlow's experiment). He seeks admiration and adoration. Therefore, the dynamics are different. He needs applause, medals, prizes, he needs to be told he is wonderful, great, strong; he has to maintain a grandiose self. Therefore, he is not interested in what happens to others but only in their adoration of him.

This pattern is illustrated by the following example. When Charles Manson was in jail after the murders, he received thousands of letters from people supporting him and identifying with him. Manson answered them: "People need God, God does not need people."[59] Manson, as God in a prison cell, really does not need anyone.

The above discussion raises questions regarding the generalization of these arguments. We are dealing here with outstanding leaders and not with a representative sample. Furthermore, writing and research on leadership almost always deals with exceptional people, particularly those who are of interest to particular scholars, or scholars who are interested in specific aspects. This further complicates the issue of generalization of arguments concerning leaders.

Freud himself referred to this matter and its implications in 1933, in an introduction to Marie Bonaparte's book on Edgar Allen Poe. He wrote: "There is a special attraction in learning about human thought as manifested by *exceptional* people" [italics added] (p. 254).[60]

This was not the first time Freud had expressed such an idea. Twenty years earlier he was intrigued by the work and achievements of Leonardo da Vinci, who was an exceptional person by every criterion. Freud (perhaps because he himself was a genius) wanted very much to know what motivated "a man of genius" (Freud's definition), such as da Vinci, to function as he did. He wanted to find the key to da Vinci's intellectual development and to analyze and characterize his personality in clinical terms.

Freud's study on da Vinci became a model for later psychobiographies. For example, Stefan Zweig and Lytton Strachey were strongly influenced by Freud's approach. Referring to this, McAdams[61] said: "The biographer's task has changed from lavishing praise to psychological analysis" (p. 3). This type of writing and analysis was perceived as an "educational mission," a service to the public to improve their criteria for evaluating leaders. Mack[62] expressed this attitude in a most judgmental way: "Research on political leaders and on those who seek power can contribute to the body of public knowledge, which may ultimately lead to more rational judgments on the part of those citizens who wish to control their own fate" (p. 177).

Apparently this approach led to the emphasis on psychopathological aspects. A sample review of the better-known studies that were conducted from this viewpoint will testify to the possible validity of the argument presented here. The first study of leaders written from a psychodynamic perspective was by Lasswell[63] in 1930. He claims that political leaders displace their personal whims to public objects and then rationalize this as the public interest. Another study mentioned earlier in this book, whose authors were deeply influenced by Laswell's analysis, is George and George's work on Woodrow Wilson.[64] Wilson is presented as a man whose motivation for public activity originated from his personal need for strength to compensate him for his miserable childhood with his father. Two famous works that present similar arguments are by the eminent psychologist Erik Erikson, who left a clear stamp on psychological theory. He examines the lives of Martin Luther[65] and Mahatma Gandhi,[66] and he, too, shows how personal identity crises are displaced to the public level.

It seems to me that these few references provide sufficient evidence for the caution with which we must relate to generalizations on leaders. Furthermore, these examples also indicate that some of the writers may have been influenced by each other, which of course strengthens the possible bias.

CHAPTER 2

THE FUEL

Hypnotized Followers

When everyone thinks the same way—no-one is thinking.

Walter Lippmann

THE TALE OF A FEEBLE-MINDED GARDENER

Chauncey was a simple man; in fact, he was mentally retarded. All he knew about himself were two facts: He was an orphan, and he worked as a gardener on the estate of an old man. His daily life consisted of taking care of the garden and watching television. Everything he knew about the outside world came from compulsively watching, without distinction or understanding, an endless variety of TV programs.

One day his patron, the old man, died and Chauncey was thrown into the world outside the estate. Until then, his patron had protected him and prevented him from being committed to an institution; now he was left without protection. Chauncey stepped outside the grounds of the estate for the first time and was hit by a limousine. As he was only slightly injured, the limousine's owner, Mrs. Rand, wife of the chairman of a huge American corporation, took him to her house. She was soon deeply impressed by his rare intelligence and insight, as she said. In fact, the only thing that Chauncey did in his conversations with Mrs. Rand was to repeat what she said—a response he had learned from one of the TV programs he watched.

Mrs. Rand was not the only one to be deeply impressed by the feeble-minded gardener. Her husband, a businessman with a finger in every pie, was also impressed by Chauncey's wisdom. When Rand asked Chauncey about his business (because obviously such a clever man must be in business), the conversation between them went as follows: "It's not easy, sir," said Chauncey, "There are not many chances of getting a good garden where you can work undisturbed and cultivate it according to the changing seasons." Mr. Rand leaned toward him smugly and said, "Extremely well put, a gardener, uh? Isn't that a wonderfully apt description of a true businessman? A person who tills the soil with his sweat, waters the ground and harvests from it worthwhile products for his family, his community. Yes, Chauncey! What a wonderful metaphor! Indeed, a productive businessman is like a man of the soil cultivating his vine."[1]

The process of attributing superior wisdom to Chauncey, the ignorant gardener, gathered speed. The president of the United States visited Rand's house and spoke with Chauncey. He took the opportunity to ask Chauncey's opinion on the rough period in the U.S. economy. Chauncey answered, "There are always seasons in gardening. There is spring, there is summer, but there is also fall and winter, and then again spring and summer. So long as the roots are not seriously damaged, everything is all right."

The president took Chauncey's answer as one of the wisest and most optimistic statements he had ever heard and began to use the "seasons" metaphor in his speeches at the Senate.

From then on, things snowballed. One thing led to another, and Chauncey suddenly found himself appearing on TV shows. Introducing the program, the host would state that the U.S. president compared the American economy to a garden. Chauncey, when invited to speak, simply recited the only thing he knew and had done all his life: "I know the garden well," he said firmly, "I have worked at this job all my life, the good, healthy garden. The trees are healthy, and so are the flowers and the other plants. And they will stay that way if they are watered and treated properly according to the seasons of the year. The garden needs proper care! I agree very much with the U.S. president. There is room for new trees and new flowers of different kinds. . . ." And so Chauncey went on, describing the garden he had worked in on the old man's estate: "In the garden the plants grow, but you also have to go through the fall, the trees shed their leaves and their color changes. It is a stage in the process of becoming taller and thicker. True, some branches die, but others grow in their place. If you like the garden it is not hard to wait. And then, in the right season, you see the blossom." The audience responded enthusiastically to Chauncey's profound words. They all wanted to meet him, to get to know him. When he laughed for no rhyme or reason at a reception given by the Russian ambassador, the latter immediately suspected that Chauncey knew Russian and had overheard a joke someone had told in that language. When he was asked by a journalist which newspapers he preferred to read, Chauncey replied that he did not read any paper (he could not read or write). "I watch TV programs all the time," he said spontaneously. His reply came across as one of the most honest answers ever uttered by a public figure: He did not try to improve his image in order to impress. In the same way, when he responded to a publisher's invitation to write a book with "I can't write," "Who can today? Who has time for it?" said the publisher, delighted with the honest and genuine reply and at once offered him a ghost writer from the publishing house. Asked about subjects such as industrial waste and the effect of certain substances on the environment, he replied that chemical substances harm the plants in the garden. Chauncey's ability to express complex subjects in a simple way captivated everybody. The president wanted to know more about him, fashion magazines ranked him as a very elegant man, all the newspapers rushed to print front page articles about him, and the leaders of a certain political party saw him as a possible candidate to lead the party forward.

This is how the Polish-American author Jerzy Kozinski brilliantly portrayed people's subjective need to create a leader for themselves in his book *Being There*.

"YOU HAVE A MANTLE, YOU SHALL BE OUR LEADER"

This example is fictional and satirical, but the theme—that people need a clear and comprehensible world and that this need leads them to adopt authority figures even at the expense of reality—has been known since ancient times ("You have a mantle, you shall be our leader," Isaiah 3:6) and has been discussed by philosophers, sociologists, anthropologists, and psychologists. This is the point of departure for the discussion on the influence of leaders in general and hypnotic leaders in particular. Their influence was not created out of thin air: It was planted in fertile soil, it answered people's expectations and yearnings, their readiness to accept—and even create—them. From this point of departure, we will examine and illustrate the various explanations of the emotional need for a leader.

The first group of explanations is derived from psychoanalytic theory. People's emotional need, even yearning, for leaders can be explained with the help of two concepts: "transference" and "projection." Transference is a central concept in psychoanalytic practice. Freud explains it as follows (in a clinical context): "The patient sees in [the analyst] the return, the reincarnation, of some important figure out of his childhood or past, and consequently transfers on to him feelings and reactions which undoubtedly applied to his prototype" (p. 174).[2]

Thus, transference does not relate only to people in the here and now, but also, unconsciously, to figures from the past. In the therapeutic situation, the interaction between therapist and client includes feelings and attitudes toward authority figures from the past that are transferred to the therapist although they are not really connected with him.

The extension of this argument to the constant yearning for authority figures, for leaders, stems from the basic transference argument as formulated by Freud himself: "People have a strong need for authority that can be admired, to which we can bow, by which we are ruled. From individual psychology we have learned what is the source of this need. It is the yearning for a father that everyone feels from childhood on."[3]

Thus, according to Freud, at the unconscious level, leaders represent the primeval father. The emotional attraction to them and the surrender to their authority provide a solution to powerful emotional conflicts and tensions. As with the original Oedipal conflict, when the child finally accepts the father's authority and identifies with it, and thereby solves his raging emotions and his feelings of guilt for desiring his mother and competing for her, a similar thing happens when followers accept the authority of leaders. Moreover, identifying with them has a very releasing effect on the followers. Kets de Vries, one of the better known researchers on leadership,[4] claims, on the basis of his observations, that this emotional function of the leader can easily create euphoria among the led. Like the solution to the original Oedipal conflict, identification with the leader releases worried feelings caused by various prohibitions. (This seems to be reflected in the type of argument used by officers and members of the Nazi regime, including Adolf Eichmann when he said at his trial, "I didn't think, there was a leader, I just obeyed orders." Identification with the leader frees the follower of the need to hesitate, consider options, take a stand. Obedience is the easy way out.)

Another psychodynamic explanation of the need for leaders, for the emotional attachment to leaders, is projection. Projection refers to the tendency to see others through oneself, through the subjective spectacles that express one's yearnings, wishes, and desires. In other words, the other is the screen onto which the individual projects his own characteristics, which often have no real connection with the object of the projection. The projective explanations relevant to the discussion on emotional attachment to leaders relate mainly to projections whose source is narcissistic.[5] Kohut and Winnicott describe how the baby in his early developmental stages is enchanted by his own grandiosity. His parents adore him. To them (like most parents), he is an unparalleled wonder. They hover round him, stroke and kiss him, react to every flutter of his eyelashes and every murmur. The baby is in fact omnipotent, he can move all the world that he is capable of containing (through hearing, touching, seeing). Thus, his primary feeling is that he is the world and the world is him. He is at its center. Nothing can be compared with this feeling, which will never return in later stages of his life. Shamir, referring to leader-follower relations, says "It is the search for 'lost paradise' that causes subordinates to make the leader the recipient of their own desire for grandiosity. Through vicarious identification and projection processes, the leaders become the recipients (containers) of the followers' ideals, wishes, desires, and fantasies. Thus the attachment to charismatic leadership is a manifestation of the desire for narcissistic unity, formed first from self-love, and then from love of idealized others who promise a return to that unity" (p. 85).[6]

There are other variations of the projection explanation, but their underlying logic is similar. The important point for our discussion is that both the projective-narcissistic explanation and the transference explanation indicate an attachment whose sources stem from early childhood, that is to say, an attachment that is essentially regressive; in other words, an attachment that has nothing to do with the content, the message, or the quality of the idea that the leader represents. These primary yearnings are entirely process-related and are devoid of any critical approach to content. The attraction to leaders stems from what they represent at the level of the unconscious and not from the contents of their statement or their struggle.

Explanations that are essentially similar, referring to unconscious and uncontrolled primary emotions, have been offered in professional literature on "mass psychology." Some of the outstanding scholars in the field of mass psychology are Mesmer,[7] Le Bon,[8] and Tarde.[9] The masses, according to these writers, constitute an entity in itself. This entity is not a "moral authority" or a spontaneous form but a phenomenon that precedes every social order and thought. It is an amorphous mass of meaningless desires. The image used by these writers in describing the nature of the masses is "hypnotic." The hypnotic state, they say, is an everyday state in which the individual finds himself, particularly in mass situations. As Tarde says (p. 77): "The social like the hypnotic state is only a form of dream, a dream of command."

Like the psychodynamic explanations dealing with the individual and the leader, this explanation is rooted in irrational worlds of desires, feelings, lack of control, and so forth, but the focus of discussion is the masses. The assumption is that the masses have an effect that exists in its own right. In other words, they are not simply a collection of individuals but an entity with its own psychology and dynamics. When such an entity comes into being, the conditions are created for emotional processes that are aptly described by the word hypnosis, and then leaders can be hypnotists.

Finally, another explanation for the followers' longing, which may explain the emotional dependence on leaders but is not based on regressive desires and unconscious primeval forces, is related to the psychological phenomenon known as attribution. Research on attribution has produced an abundance of arguments and findings. To put it simply, these studies seek to find the patterns, the regularity of explanations that people give to themselves concerning phenomena, or they seek connections between phenomena. The assumption is that just as scientists and researchers form hypotheses and attempt to examine and verify them, people who are not researchers intuitively think in the same way. Researchers on attribution try to find the regularity of the type of thinking with regard to the way in which people explain the world to themselves, and the behaviors that occur in the world (this refers, of course, to social behaviors). For example, a greater tendency was found for people to attribute successes to themselves (this is defined in the literature as "internal attribution") and to attribute failures to external factors such as bad luck, injustice of the system, and so forth ("external attribution").

An error of attribution that is very relevant in explaining the empowerment of leaders (from the point of view of the followers) is the bias known as "fundamental attribution error." This bias, which has been studied in the field of cognitive psychology, describes people's tendency to see behavior as arising from the characteristics of the one performing the actions and ignore the effect of situational factors. The example usually cited to illustrate this basic argument refers to a teacher who is angry with his students. Onlookers will tend to see him as bad-tempered and irritable, usually without considering the circumstances of the case. A well-known experiment by Ross and colleagues[10] illustrates the power of the fundamental attribution error. They conducted a quiz in which their subjects were divided arbitrarily into questioners and respondents. The questioners were instructed to find hard questions and put them to the respondents. The questioner was entitled by virtue of his role to ask questions on subjects to which nobody could possibly know the answer. An audience watched the distribution of roles and the quiz; they knew that the role distribution was random. Nevertheless, they attributed greater knowledge to the questioner than to the respondent, ignoring the simple fact that the questioner's advantage stemmed solely from his appointed role. In other words, anyone could have successfully filled the role of questioner and gained the same advantage.

Interesting examples of the fundamental attribution error can also be found outside the context of laboratory experiments. For example, it was found that there is a clear tendency to blame drivers for road accidents and underrate the effect of defects in infrastructure, roads, road signs, condition of the vehicles, and such.[11] The researchers found that there is a tendency to focus attention on the "acting person" and not on what is around him. This finding is relevant to the argument concerning the empowerment of leaders and reduction of the importance of situational background factors. These are also the findings of Conger and Kanungo,[12] two well-known scholars who studied the question of attribution in relation to leaders. They found a strong tendency to attribute to people who behaved in a way appropriate to leaders (determination, firmness, and so on) not only leadership but, in their words, "charismatic leadership."

In a paper that presents another way of looking at leader-led relations, Shamir, House, and Arthur[13] present a different model from the regressive psychodynamic one. This model serves as the basis for other predictions regarding the emotional relationship between the led and leaders. Following are the assumptions underlying their proposed model:

1. People are not only practical or oriented towards their aims, they also have a need for self-expression.

2. People are motivated to preserve and promote their sense of self-esteem and self-worth.

3. People are motivated to preserve and increase their self-consistency, that is, consistency between their beliefs about themselves and their actions.

4. Self-perceptions are partly composed of identities. Identities are organized in the self-perception in a hierarchy of prominence.[14] The more prominent the identity, the stronger its significance as a motivating need.

The emotional attachment to leaders develops, according to Shamir and his colleagues, because certain leaders are associated in the awareness of their followers with those aspects of value in their own self-perception, and thus they harness the motivating powers of self-expression, self-consistency, self-esteem, and self-worth.

On the basis of this argument, leaders have a different function from that ascribed to them by the process-oriented explanations hitherto emphasized. According to the process-oriented explanations, the leader, whether he represents a father figure or someone who "knows the way," whether he is a "focus of narcissistic projections" or a "hypnotic medium," serves to *alleviate a distressing emotional process*, which is painful and demanding and, as we have seen, often threatening. The attachment to the leader is based entirely on dynamics of self-loss. In contrast, Shamir and his colleagues' argument is content-oriented, not process-oriented.

Leaders, explain Shamir and his colleagues, may represent a certain content in the components of the followers' identity—an identity that includes prominent and conscious components that are knowingly adopted and controlled by the individual. Simply put, the individual is not swallowed up in the figure of the leader because that is a way of escaping distress; on the contrary, the leader is put to a test derived from the identity of the individual. He has to meet the criteria of the follower in terms of ideas and content. This argument attributes a great deal of weight to the follower, to his judgment, his maturity, and his rounded identity. Inherent in this argument is an assumption that followers choose who will represent their inner being. There are, indeed, researchers who refer to the existence of schemata of leadership[15] among the led, saying that leaders are accepted or rejected according to their compatibility with these schemata. A democrat will seek compatibility with a democratic view, and so forth. This approach reverses the argument concerning the great power of leaders, saying that it is the followers who, in fact, carry the greatest weight in determining leadership. To stretch the argument even further, the leaders are merely extensions of the followers.

The two basic approaches presented here, one attributing exclusive weight to the leaders and the other ascribing exclusive weight to the followers, are diametrically opposed and both ignore the circumstances, the actual cultural context, of the processes of influence. The ensuing discussion will deal with the interactions between the different components, attempting to determine which of the two approaches is more valid in explaining situations in which the leader appears huge and the follower tiny. In such situations, the leader has vast powers, yet it all takes place in the followers' subjective scenario, where every definition is based on extremely powerful emotions. This is the point of departure for the attempt to understand the influence of particularly charismatic leaders, leaders who are often hypnotic.

CHAPTER 3

THE FIRE

Leaders, Followers, and Circumstances

In times of trouble people tend more to believe in gods.
                                                    Lucretius

When a person needs to believe in something, facts will not make
him budge from his opinion.
                                                    Nathan Shacham

Absolute faith destroys like absolute power.
                                                    Erik Hoffer

THE MEETING OF THE SPARK, THE FUEL,
AND THE OXYGEN

Nothing could be more apposite to the discussion of leadership
than the image formulated by Klein and House:[1] the leader is the
"spark," the followers are the "fuel," and the circumstances are the
"oxygen." All three components create and maintain the "fire."
Fire is an apt metaphor for the phenomenon of leadership: It can be
pleasant and warming, it can fade slowly, it can die suddenly, or it
can blaze up and destroy everything in its path. Another thing,
anyone who has sat near a fireplace or a bonfire knows that hyp-

notic feeling of gazing into the dancing flames. You can sit for hours, hypnotized by the flames.

The interplay of the three components that create fire (spark, fuel, and oxygen) provides an appropriate conceptual framework for analyzing the dynamics of leadership in an attempt to understand the relative weight of each component and the process by which leaders' power and influence grow. This conceptual framework can also serve in the comparative analysis of leadership in various contexts of circumstances and followers. Some of the more vexing questions can, I believe, be discussed more analytically in this framework. For example, was the rise of Hitler and his leadership a function of circumstances at a certain point in history, or could this phenomenon only have occurred in a certain society? Is it possible that in certain contexts every collective will behave in the way described by Le Bon, Tarde, and others—with instinctive, hypnotic, herdlike behavior? Could leaders like Hitler have the same kind of influence in other circumstances, among followers with different cultural and psychological characteristics? Questions such as these can be analyzed more richly and precisely using the metaphor of leadership as fire created by the three components of spark, fuel, and oxygen.

I have stressed this point here because most writers on leadership, as we shall see below, usually emphasize just one of the three components. For many years, research on leadership concentrated on the leaders' influence. As the scope of leadership research developed, more attention was paid to situational and contextual factors, and in recent years, attention has focused on the followers. However, it is rare to find systematic analysis dealing with the overall nature of the dynamic interaction of these three components and attempting to explain how this gestalt called leadership is formed.

The descriptions that appear in the earlier chapters of this book suffer from the same inadequacy and should thus be seen for the moment as a partial and disproportional analysis, which overemphasizes psychodynamic personality aspects. Having voiced these reservations, I shall now attempt to discuss the subject in the metaphoric context of leadership as fire, and this, I hope, will permit me to develop a more comprehensive argument. First, let us review briefly those biases in analysis that I have referred to, in order to illustrate the development of thought regarding leadership up to the point of departure that opened this chapter.

The first modern attempt to formulate a theory of leadership appears to be that of Thomas Carlyle, a Scottish philosopher, who presented his theory in 1841.[2] According to Carlyle, "History is merely the biography of leaders." Carlyle ascribes the entire phenomenon of leadership to the leader himself. It is he who leads the masses, who creates history and society, who molds the masses in his own image. He claims that general history, the chronicles of all the deeds performed by man on earth, is essentially the chronicles of the great people who acted in it. Those great people were the leaders of people. They were the ones who created everything that humanity enacted.

The leader's influence, according to Carlyle, is not limited to the social and political level. He is above all a spiritual leader and, therefore, Carlyle numbers among his heroes leaders and prophets whose outstanding characteristic is genius. Carlyle's hero stands above others in his purity, courage, originality, and ability to see the truth.

This romantic, one-dimensional approach came to characterize the point of departure for scientific research on leadership. The first empirical treatment of the subject was called the "trait approach," and was based on the assumption (like Carlyle's) that the leader is a person gifted with exceptional qualities by virtue of which he exerts his influence. The first study conducted according to this orientation was by Terman (1904),[3] who tried to identify characteristics of student leaders by observations in schools as well as reports by teachers and students. The findings of this experiment did, in fact, indicate that the leaders located through the researcher's observation were the same as those identified as such by their friends and teachers. The leaders' characteristics, as identified, indicated that they surpassed their friends in size, style of dress, daring, eloquence, personal appearance, and reading habits.

After Terman's experiment, studies of this type were increasingly conducted, in different variations and more complex research designs. In 1948, Stogdill[4] could already review 140 studies on leadership examining dozens of traits that were supposed to distinguish leaders from others. Some of the studies following Terman examined physical traits such as outward appearance or height; others examined such features as intelligence, determination, originality, and so forth. Many of these studies contradict each other: Traits that were identified in one study did not appear in others, and altogether no clear and comprehensive statement can be made about the characteristics of leaders on the basis of these empirical studies. This approach, based on the belief that leaders' qualities are inherent, lost its central place in leadership research, although there are still studies on leaders' traits (though not necessarily inborn), for example, networking skills, the ability to tolerate frustration, and the like, which emphasize characteristics that can be acquired and developed.[5] One way or another, after decades of research focusing on leaders alone, it became clear that neither psychological and philosophical thought nor scientific research can explain leadership by referring exclusively to leaders.

Karl Marx and, perhaps even more, his friend and student Friedrich Engels represent a diametrically opposed approach to Carlyle's view of the leader as the be-all and end-all, the view of the "great man," the trait approach, and all the other expressions used in explaining events solely by the leaders' qualities and deeds. Engels totally negates the importance attributed to the leader's personality and characteristics, seeing this as merely a chance component in the development of processes that would have occurred anyway. He argues that it is pure accident that a particular personality and not another appears in a certain period in a certain country. But if we take away this accident, the need will arise to fill the same place, and in time somebody will be found to fill this role somehow. It was not by chance that Napoleon, that particular Corsican, became a military dictator who was needed for the battle-weary French republic. But if there had been no Napoleon, someone else would have taken his place. And the proof of this is that whenever there was a need, the suitable person was found—Caesar, Augustus, Cromwell, and so on.[6]

Marx himself never dealt directly with the question of leaders' personalities. In his view, "circumstances" are the decisive factor, not the "great man." Marx believed in the existence of a historical order that is socioeconomic, not spiritual-mystic. It is the circumstances that dictate events, so that the leaders, whatever their characteristics, are bound by circumstances whose dialectics dictate development. He claimed that people create their own history, but they create it not just as they imagine it, not in circumstances they choose for themselves, but in circumstances they find facing them directly.[7]

The dialectical approach to leadership, first expressed in philosophical thought, was translated into empirical research that emerged after the disappointment with the trait approach. Now the emphasis in research shifted to the situation or circumstances as the major factor explaining events that were hitherto explained solely through the leader.

A typical example of research based on the "situational approach" is a study by Leavitt,[8] examining the effect on leadership positions of various seating arrangements (different situations) in a group. Subjects taking part in discussion groups were seated artificially in arrangements that gave certain individuals advantages in communication. For example, in a Y arrangement, the person sitting at the center of the Y, where the three branches meet, can control the communication because all the communication in the group must go through him. After a time, those individuals who were placed at the center tended to adopt leadership-type behavior.

This research approach was regarded as limited and technical, an approach that might produce results in laboratory conditions but could contribute nothing to the explanation of leadership in real circumstances. Furthermore, the criticism of such research was part of a generally critical approach toward the behavioral and social sciences' adoption of the forms of thinking and research methods of the life sciences. One of the major critics was the German sociologist Max Weber. According to him, research in the social sciences cannot be based on the discovery of objective, predictable laws through impartial observation. The methodology of the social sciences is based, in Weber's view, on observation of an entity that by its very definition has subjective dimensions and, therefore, has to take into consideration the subjective meanings, the intentions/interpretations of the participants in a given social situation. Weber thus provided an important contribution to the discussion on leadership (especially through the term he dealt with: "charisma"), expanding the explanation of the leadership phenomenon to include the *followers' perceptions* as a point of departure. According to this point of departure, the charismatic leader is the one who is perceived by those who follow him as having exceptional, sometimes even superhuman, qualities and as someone bearing a new message.

Weber's emphasis on the followers' subjective perception of their leader represents a totally different attitude from that of Carlyle and others who study traits, who see the leader as someone possessing outstanding objective qualities, the qualities of a genius. In Weber's view, the followers are the ones who determine the leader's size and characteristics. He states that the leader's charismatic call collapses if his mission is not recognized by those to whom he is called according to his inner feeling. If they recognize him, he is their master, as long as he knows how to achieve their recognition that he will prove himself.[9]

Weber's thinking contributed greatly to the development of research that views leadership as interaction between leaders and followers. According to this view, neither the leaders' traits nor the followers' perception of them explain the phenomenon, but some kind of interaction (whose foundations are subjective) is what explains why a certain individual will be perceived and accepted as a leader, while another (who would very much like to be a leader) will not be acclaimed by the people. This interaction, as later research showed, may also be affected by the circumstances, which in their turn affect the expectations underlying the interaction between a leader and his followers. A historical example, perhaps the most outstanding one, that illustrates the dynamics of leader, followers, and circumstances is the rise and fall of Winston Churchill as Britain's national leader in World War II. In early May 1940, after the defeat in Norway, the British felt that Prime Minister Chamberlain was not a suitable leader in wartime. Chamberlain resigned and his place was taken by Churchill, who until then had been considered an erratic adventurer but was now perceived by the English as a suitable leader for that time. But after the war, when the circumstances changed radically, the English public did not elect Churchill, the revered leader of the war period. Instead, they elected Clement Attlee, a much less impressive personality, who was perceived as a suitable leader for the new circumstances of peace and economic recovery.

Empirical research also gave expression to this development. Hollander[10] saw leadership as transaction and formulated the leader's position in his followers' eyes in terms of credit (idiosyncratic credit, in his definition). For example, if a leader accumulates successes and meets expectations at the beginning of his way, he acquires credit in his followers' eyes, but this credit can disappear if he does not meet their expectations over a period of time. An illustration of this argument is the acceptance of Israel's late prime minister, Yitzhak Rabin, as a national leader. His service as a commander in the Palmach (the pre-State military force that fought in the War of Independence) and as chief of staff during the Six Day War gave him credit with the public, and this credit was transformed into political capital, although political leadership is not necessarily a natural continuation of military leadership.

Some of the major researchers of this approach, which is known as contingency theory, are Fiedler,[11] Reddin,[12] and Vroom and Yetton,[13] who present a model that includes leaders, followers, and circumstances. These social scientists differ from each other in the weight they attribute to each of the components, but there is no doubt that their work contributed substantially to the systematic study of the complex phenomenon of leadership.

However, their approach, despite its conceptual importance and fruitfulness for research, tends to blur the uniqueness of the leadership phenomenon. It is hard to discern whether the leader is merely one who responds to expectations and the challenges of the task or whether he makes a larger contribution. Perhaps he is the one who formulates the expectations. Perhaps he also shapes the circumstances. Or does he just shape himself according to the circumstances? Is the leader's outstanding quality mere adaptability, flexibility? Something fundamental in the intuitive context of the term "leadership" seems to get lost in the approaches represented by Fiedler, Reddin, and others. Although their studies deal with the leader, the followers, and the circumstances, the active aspect of leadership is blurred, if not lost entirely, and without this active element there is no fire.

It is only in the last two decades, particularly in the 1980s, that the leader has been restored to his former glory, but this is not a return to Carlyle's ideas but to the concept of the "transformational leader." The idea is that although the choice and acceptance of a leader are affected by the followers' perceptions and expectations in given circumstances, the leader has enough space to influence his followers' expectations. He can shape them, he can transform their expectations *from his leadership position*. Briefly, he can be active and he can lead.

The eminent proponents of this approach are James Macgregor Burns, a political historian who coined the term "transformational leadership,"[14] and Bernard Bass,[15] a psychologist who was deeply influenced by Burns and developed a methodology and research tools to measure Burns's concepts, particularly in small groups and organizations. This view casts a different light on the dynamics of the components of leadership. If we return to the example of Churchill, although the circumstances and the followers played a decisive part in the actual choice, in the fact of his acceptance as a leader, from that point on it was Churchill himself who shaped the expectations of the British. He projected expectations, transmitted messages, demanded "blood, sweat and tears"; he was active, he led, he was a leader. Only when the circumstances changed radically did his acceptance by the people come to an end, and the ability to lead, to influence, and to shape was taken from him.

The current literature distinguishes between two leadership patterns. One is leadership based entirely on the idea of exchange

between leader and followers; in other words, a transaction between two sides acting to fulfill their mutual expectations. This pattern is called "transactional leadership." The other pattern,
described by Burns and Bass, is known as "transformational leadership," wherein the leader's ability to shape or transform his followers' expectations goes beyond the regular limits of a transaction.

THE CONFLAGRATION

Before discussing how the meeting between leader and followers develops until it bursts into flame, we need to be aware that
leadership relations are not all the same and cannot be discussed as
one uniform thing. Just as situations differ, leadership relations
may be rooted in different dynamics.

An important distinction that is relevant here is the difference
between leadership in everyday life—such as between a manager
and his staff, a teacher and his students, or perhaps the most common, between a parent and his children—and leadership in times
of crisis.

The two patterns—transactional leadership and transformational
leadership—may be found in the dynamics of leadership in everyday life. The transactional pattern, as stated, is based on exchange
relations: The assumption is that the participants on both sides
have clear motivations and expectations, which are the basis for
give-and-take relations between the leader and his followers. This
may be described as a relationship between adults, based first and
foremost on the participants' ability to define their wishes and expectations in order to maintain the transaction and the motivation
required to fill their side of the "bargain." This is the common pattern of relations in business organizations. The effective
transactional leader is the one who succeeds in creating a close link
between effort and reward in the followers' awareness. (The reward is not necessarily material; it may be psychological.)

In transformational leadership, the relations between the leader
and his people are different. In this pattern, which can be compared

to the relationship between good parents and their children, the developmental aspect is central.

The transformational leader motivates his people not to remain content with their present and immediate expectations. He motivates them to strive for self-fulfillment at a higher level, to think in more ideological terms, to think and behave more morally, to expand their view from narrow self-interest to broader horizons.

The dynamics that characterize both patterns of leadership are not necessarily those that will exist in crisis situations. A crisis situation may change the expectations of all those involved, as described by scholars of leadership such as Heifetz[16] and Lindholm.[17] According to process-oriented psychodynamic explanations, in crisis situations the instinctive, unconscious longing for authority, for a dominant father figure, as described by Freud, comes to the fore. Briefly, people tend to unconsciously seek the kind of relationships that psychoanalyst Kets de Vries,[18] a researcher on leadership, called regressive relations. In such cases, there is heightened probability of that psychological condition defined by Lindholm[19] as self-loss—a condition of total merging with the figure of the leader and loss of autonomous judgment. How does this happen? What forces are at work in these situations? What characterizes these extreme changes in awareness and behavior? Many books and plays have been written dealing with these questions of merging with others, loss of autonomous judgment, self-loss. For example, Durenmatt's famous play *The Visit of the Old Lady* is about an old lady who was abandoned as a young girl in the village by her lover, and who returns decades later as a rich woman to take revenge on him. The plot describes a process that begins with the villagers' determined defense of their friend (the lady's one-time lover) and ends with their total surrender to her demands and abandonment of their friend. The villagers' gradual change of attitudes, until they finally adopt an attitude that would not have seemed possible at the beginning of the play, is portrayed in a way that makes the flesh creep. The play's powerful effect is reflected in the audience's wondering: Would I, too, gradually develop a rhinoceros hide and behave the same way in those circumstances? This question has triggered dramas, books, plays, and films dealing with subjects of this nature. Yet surprisingly few attempts have been made to study the psychological processes at the basis of these happenings. Beyond a few testimonies and papers written in special and distinct circumstances, these psychological processes have not been examined in the context of leaders' influence. Therefore, I will first present examples to illustrate what I call "change of awareness," and then I will discuss this in the overall framework of leadership.

One example of "natural laboratory conditions," which are, of course, exceptional, for the examination of the phenomenon of extreme changes of awareness was exploited in a fascinating way by Schein, Schnier, and Barker,[20] who became interested in the subject of brainwashing following the Korean War. The term "brainwashing" was first coined in 1951 by Edward Hunter,[21] who examined processes of persuasion in Communist China. Schein and his colleagues conducted their research among a group of Americans and Europeans, businessmen, doctors, and students who were in Beijing when the Korean War broke out. They were arrested and imprisoned for three to five years, and when they were released, they uttered statements such as, "There are no false imprisonments in China," "They put no pressure on us," "I knew I was guilty but I could not admit it," and so forth. Their attitudes had changed so radically that it was clear they had been brainwashed. The research attempted to examine what had happened, how this influence had been created, and how such a strong effect had been achieved. For this purpose, the researchers read analyses written by Russians and Chinese, read autobiographies of prisoners and others, and interviewed Americans who had undergone processes described by an eminent researcher in the field, Robert Lifton,[22] as "thought reform." All these materials pointed to a number of possible explanations, most of them revolving around manipulation of the identity. The explanations emphasize different factors, but the undermining of the identity and the criticality and fragility of what is called the sense of self pass like a silken thread through most of the explanations. In his influential work,[23] Lifton describes in detail the techniques and procedures used in the process of thought reform.

These include humiliation that is later associated with expressions of friendship and help, public confessions of past psychological conditions, arousal of guilt feelings, and peer group pressure.

Constant massive repetition of such procedures leads to disintegration of the identity, regression to infantile states, and states of dependency, which are the basis for dramatic changes in the personality. According to Lifton's findings, a process of psychological regression occurs, but rather than keeping the subject arrested in a state of apathy, it generates personality changes with a salient emotional element. The result is an altered state of consciousness. Out of the humiliation, pain, and stress, a peak experience is born, one of release from the constraints of human ambivalence, from the restrictions of what is "wrong" and what is "right," release from guilt of all kinds. People undergoing this process are enveloped in a transcendental feeling of absolute truth, of unquestioning faith, unlike anything they have ever felt before. According to all the evidence of people who have undergone these processes, it is a "wonderful feeling."[24] This is the basis for those seemingly incomprehensible phenomena that psychologists call "identification with the aggressor." Prisoners of war identifying with their captors, people internalizing ideologies they had fought to suppress, or totally justifying the enemies' actions—all these are examples of the results of thought reform. The evidence cited by Lifton, Hunter, and Schein indicates that this can be a mass phenomenon, and indeed the phenomena and processes described by Lifton and his colleagues are similar to the hypnotic effect described by Le Bon, Tarde, and others in *Mass Psychology*. Controlled laboratory experiments have also shown in detail the meanings of those "altered states of consciousness induced by laboratory manipulation."[25] In these experiments, which included both tests and self-reports by the subjects, it was found that the shift to altered states of consciousness was characterized by a return to those primary processes described by Freud: states in which the link between cause and effect is blurred, the ambiguity and confusion are enormous, the usual rationality is pushed aside, and the consciousness is marked by delusions. In addition, the sense of time is lost, and all this is accompanied by blurring of the borders between the self and the surroundings. Almost paradoxically, as the participants describe in their reports, the loss of rationality and the growth of delusions lead to a feeling of ecstasy and euphoria. They have a sense of grandiosity and feel that they possess enormous power.

Many studies have shown a significant correlation between the length of time a person is in an altered state of consciousness and permanent changes in his personality. As one researcher described it: "The disappearance of control over the consciousness and inhibitions is accompanied by changes in the emotional expression. Then primitive feelings arise with much greater intensity than in a normal state of consciousness."[26] Thus, we are now able to describe how such psychological processes occur. We have descriptions of research, experiments, evidence from the field, as well as historical events, and we can characterize the phenomena and describe their manifestations in precise detail. The answer to the question, What happens? seems much clearer today.

But why does it happen? How can we explain the deep internal processes that underlie the outward symptoms? This is a more complex question. Almost certainly, as Schein argues, there is not one single explanation that can account for all these extreme psychological phenomena. Apparently several explanations are needed here.

To analyze the forces that work to alter consciousness in general, and the fire kindled between leader, followers, and circumstances, Kurt Lewin's "field force theory"[27] seems to offer an appropriate framework. According to Lewin, reality is a field of forces acting to preserve the status quo or to change it. A change in attitudes, for example, becomes possible when there is a change in the field forces. The forces that block change diminish, or the forces that promote change grow stronger, or both things happen together. When one of these possibilities occurs, a movement of change begins. The forces that worked to preserve the situation are no longer effective.

One type of force for altering consciousness is explained by Freudian theory, whereby the child's dependence on his parents and caregivers and the sense of helplessness connected with this dependence are a natural state, and as they grow older children learn to become independent in terms of daily functioning. However, in situations of physical and mental fatigue, uncertainty, isolation, and so forth, like those described by Schein and his colleagues with regard to prisoners of war, the adult regresses to the situation of the dependent child. One of the scholars who investigated the feasibility of total surrender to another, surrender to authority, found that the return to what he called "the natural disposition of dependency" is the psychological starting point for surrender to another.[28]

Another argument, also derived from Freudian thinking, was presented by Moloney,[29] who claims that just those people who are characterized by a strong superego (the part of the personality that represents judgment, moral imperatives, and so on) and a rather weak ego (the part of the personality that mediates between the id, the instinctive part, and the judgmental superego) are more likely to surrender to authority. Moloney reached this conclusion through his observation of cases of religious conversion. He argues that when such people live for long periods in conditions of physical and mental pressure, surrender to authority is the only substitute for suicide in order to escape the unbearable stress. Authority figures become the perfect substitute for the superego. You can surrender to them and live in a sense of absolute giving. The intolerable conflict is resolved.

Another type of explanation for the phenomenon of altered states of consciousness finds the key in the identity derived from social contact. Schein and his colleagues report that prisoners of war who were totally ignored or who spent long periods in solitary confinement actively searched for signs that would help them to organize their eroding identity. They were much more ready than others to identify with the aggressor if only they received some attention. Two eminent researchers[30,31] verified this argument in broad contexts. One of them refers to the pattern that is created by a psychosocial vacuum as "the schoolboy pattern"; that is, a subservient schoolboy who religiously and obediently learns everything he is taught, with no trace of independent thinking.

Some of the explanations that appear in the literature about processes of creating commitment are also relevant for understanding the changes of consciousness described here, particularly explanations related to cognitive dissonance theory.[32] The assumption of this theory is that the lack of compatibility between attitudes and actions (dissonance) is a distressful psychological state, and the individual, striving to achieve harmony, will attempt to rid himself of this feeling by changing either his attitudes or his behaviors. Studies dealing with this phenomenon show that it is usually the attitudes that are changed, since they are generally more amenable to change. The change of attitudes is followed by rationalization—self-justification, and only after this process is completed does the individual feel a comfortable sense of harmony between his attitudes and behaviors (consonance).

It can easily be understood from the logic of this theory that the breaking point is the critical juncture in the process of changing attitudes. At this juncture, the first crack appears between attitudes and behavior, and then the psychological mechanisms begin to work. In other words, as has been demonstrated with regard to missionaries and religious cults, the first deviant step, the first deviation from the individual's previous behaviors, creates dissonance. In this sense, the argument is that the first change in behavior is the hardest; after that, the whole process occurs much more quickly. Such observations are familiar from the behavior of people joining religious cults, of prisoners of war, and of people in "total institutions" and in military units.[33]

Lang and Lang[34] describe Billy Graham, the famous American preacher, in action. Billy Graham appeals to those who are ready "to go into details" and asks them to come up to the stage. Standing on the stage together with other witnesses, the volunteer finds himself publicly announcing that he is prepared to join the religious movement, usually without knowing what is expected of him. At the next stage in the process of creating commitment, the person is asked to sign an oath and promise to meet with representatives of the crusade or to take part in prayers that will be held at certain times. Afterward, the person signs the oath as a "witness of Jesus," and he is told that by signing he has taken an important step toward becoming part of the organization. He undertakes to adopt its values and aims, and in this way his decision becomes binding. After this, he is invited to meetings, becomes active, enjoys social support, and so forth.

This description presents the main steps in a slow process of escalating commitment to action. First, those who come to hear the preacher are people who have some inclination in that direction. The argument is, therefore, that the development of commitment, even to extreme levels, begins with a certain tendency that may or may not reach active expression but may become extreme. This is followed by a gradual process in which each stage in turn is perceived as a stable situation. At that point, nobody imagines that the situation will develop until all the earlier stages look like child's play. The initial stage has been described in psychological literature in experiments conducted to examine a model called "a foot in the door."[35] The idea is that people are asked for something small, such as Billy Graham asking people to step up to the stage. Afterward another small request is added: to sign a form. And the individual who accedes to this series of small requests thinks, "If I've already done this little thing, what does it matter if I do another little thing, it makes no difference." At a certain stage, this turns out to be a succession of steps that sometimes generates in the individual's awareness a feeling that he has reached a point of no return. From here, the distance to illogical or extreme acts may be short.

Such processes of change and readiness to see things differently from the way they are usually seen are intensified in situations of social pressure, in situations where those around become the exclusive frame of reference with regard to what is "right" or "wrong." This phenomenon has been demonstrated in many studies. An eminent scholar who was one of the first to understand processes of social influence was the social psychologist Asch.[36] In a famous experiment, he presented the participants with a visual stimulus (lines of a certain length). Before the experiment, he asked some "collaborators" to say that the lines were of a certain length that was clearly wrong. Then the participants were brought into the room and asked to state the length of the lines, after hearing the secret collaborators expressing their opinion. Although the stimulus in question was an objective visual one, most of the subjects gave the same incorrect answer that they had heard from the collaborators. When they were interviewed after the experiment and shown the true results, they said that they simply had not wanted to be different from the others although they thought that the answer was wrong. Others said that they were aware that the right answer was the one they had thought in the first place, but the answer given by the others undermined their confidence in their own judgment. Subjects from a third group denied that their answer was wrong. Their need to be part of the group was so strong that they denied even to themselves that they had been influenced by the others.

This experiment shows that people are affected in differing degrees by social pressure. At the same time, it clearly indicates that people may internalize a distorted attitude and deny the fact completely. Evidence of this is not restricted to the research laboratory. Today, there are innumerable testimonies of denial of behaviors that were deviant in every reasonable sense. Many of these testimonies were presented in courts of law as well as in historical and biographical research, and include behaviors committed during the Nazi period, for example. To anyone judging from afar, it is hard to believe, and certainly hard to understand, that this is not a question of lying but of denial so strong that the person can no longer distinguish between right and wrong.

This combination of investment (gradually created), empowerment, publicity, and social reinforcement is the foundation of the influence of leaders described here.

Kanter,[37] an American scholar who observed processes of commitment that develop in communes, found that communes create enormous commitment toward themselves, among other things because they demand sacrifice, investment of time, mental energy, and severance of previous ties—a heavy social price. Paradoxically, all this strengthens the commitment. The commune becomes a substitute for everything else, to the extent of total repudiation of personal responsibility for events. This was distinctly the case with Jim

Jones and his followers, and with Charles Manson. The same thing happened in the case of Adolf Hitler. All these cases began with a small step, followed by more steps, leading to empowerment and public investment—all the components of escalation, up to the point of no return, which was shockingly brutal. Jones and Manson themselves, according to their evidence, did not think that things would turn out that way. The escalation of the process was stronger than the participants and apparently stronger in many cases than the leader himself. He kindled the fire and, at some point, he lost control of it.

The effectiveness of forces acting to alter consciousness is not limited to frameworks that people come to by coercion. As Schein and his colleagues point out, these forces also act in frameworks that people join of their own free will. This can be seen in organizations for curing drug or alcohol addiction and even in such widespread practices as psychotherapeutic frameworks. In all these instances, powerful forces act to change the self-image, sometimes successfully. The results in these latter cases are often perceived as extremely positive, although some of the psychological mechanisms used in them are similar to those operating in cases considered distinctly negative. By including these possibilities in analyzing the dynamics of the field forces at play, we can expand the repertoire of cases of altered consciousness (beyond the moral question as to whether the change is in a good or bad direction). If we examine the phenomena in this way, we can identify conditions that promote or obstruct change of consciousness in broad frameworks beyond the family, such as groups, associations, small military units, and so forth. For example, in certain armies there is a belief that "you have to break the citizen to build a soldier." Isn't this the same as the idea at the basis of the thought reform described by Lifton? For example, in the Israeli army slang, soldiers who have deeply internalized the military values are called "poisoned." In certain cultural contexts, this poisoning is perceived as positive, but the process of poisoning people certainly contains some of the elements described above: intense social pressure, physical and mental effort that can often be justified (certainly in the case of volunteers for elite combat units) in terms of resolution of dissonance, identification with the officers who are perceived as very strong figures, in situations of fatigue, crisis, and prolonged effort. Some of the rites described in the Jim Jones cult, for example, can be identified in certain military units: intense motivation talk sessions, constant presentation of examples of good and bad behavior, incessant psychological pressure to follow the examples of good behavior in order to achieve recognition, group consultations, delegitimization of critical or deviant opinions, and so on. If a hypothetical observer of these two examples were to concentrate solely on the psychological processes involved, he would find great similarity between them. The difference, of course, lies in the direction, the content that is conveyed in these processes.

We could continue with endless models and research studies demonstrating the birth of the phenomenon in various populations and in different circumstances, but it seems to me that all the above is enough to show that people can lose their judgment, lose their inhibitions, become ready to change their opinions dramatically, and be capable of performing violent and cruel deeds without feeling any guilt. In certain cases, as a great deal of evidence indicates, those same people can simultaneously maintain loving and tender relationships with their families.

As I have shown briefly, today we can point in more detail to specific situations of such extreme changes. We see this clearly in cults such as that of Jim Jones. We are able to map more precisely the components of the environment, the characteristics of the specific population, and the nature of the particular psychological stimuli that increase dependence or the tendency for extreme change in the "potential fuel."

Although we understand the possibilities and forces acting for change of consciousness, for loss of the self, the research descriptions still relate to small frameworks. Are these precise and comprehensible descriptions of a group of prisoners or a small group of believers in a certain cult relevant also to the discussion of large societies and states?

Manson's followers shared a similar socioeconomic background and were sustained by similar motivations. The same applies to the population of Jim Jones's believers. In military units, too, especially those that become a kind of "family," a kind of cult, there is a process of self-selection.

The similarity in the effect that is generated among the followers is the basis for understanding how the fire breaks out. Such similarity is created more easily in small groups, but in some cases the similarity, the homogeneity, are not only in demographic factors such as education, economic situations, and age (a very important factor, as will be shown later). Sometimes, as is evident in extreme cults, the similarity is mainly in the followers' psychological profile, which cannot usually be identified at first glance. But a more careful analysis often reveals similarity in the parents' attitude during childhood, and a certain type of family dynamics can be discerned. In small frameworks where the followers are a more or less homogeneous group, the leader can easily maintain "charismatic relations" with all of them, both in practical and psychological terms. Furthermore, the leader can actually remove, or influence the group to remove, a follower who is not "homogeneous enough." However, when we speak of thousands, millions, of people, this is inevitably a heterogeneous population that includes every kind of difference: age, education, standard of living, family situation, and psychological personality traits. Nevertheless, Nazi Germany existed. Although the Nazi phenomenon is extreme and very distinct in human history, the fact that it existed is enough to indicate the possibility that circumstances may arise that almost obliterate the differences between people. In other words, there may be circumstances that create virtual homogeneity among the followers, or in Kurt Lewin's field force terms, circumstances that cause "melting," which brings many people who are generally very different from each other to the same psychological point of departure, the natural point of departure for the growth of hypnotic leaders.

The major circumstantial factor in creating homogeneity among the followers is the element of "crisis."[38] The central argument that appears in analyses by historians, social psychologists, and sociologists in various contexts is that the more critical the situation is perceived to be, the more the individual differences become blurred. In the context discussed here, there is a yearning for strong, perhaps transcendental, forces, and this yearning often merges with religious feelings or finds expression in the wish for a charismatic leader.

The crisis situation encompasses the instinctive emotional behavior. There are several possible explanations for the attachment to the hypnotic leader who appears in such a situation. One explanation is the constant inherent yearning for a strong man, a father. This yearning is indeed inherent, but it does not find expression in every case, only in circumstances connected entirely with the sense of loss and crisis. This longing for a leader in times of crisis was described most aptly by the wife of an American leader who was, in fact, elected during a crisis, Franklin Delano Roosevelt. This is how Eleanor Roosevelt described her husband's election in 1933, at the time of a huge economic crisis, when the banking system collapsed and uncertainty reigned in the United States: "It was quite frightening to hear that when Franklin said in his election speech that he might have to take for himself presidential powers that are generally granted to a president in wartime, just in that part of the speech he got the loudest applause."[39]

Despite this clear tendency, of which there is historical evidence, it is still not clear why a certain person succeeds in becoming the focus of collective projection, becoming the figure with whom people merge and in this way free themselves of all independent judgment.

Why did Hitler become this figure, a person who was so ridiculous, so unattractive by normal standards? Psychoanalyst David Aberbach,[40] addressed this question directly. According to his analysis, a crisis situation creates similarity between the charismatic leader's traumatic experiences and those of the collective. This similarity in traumas, in harsh experiences, makes the leader not just "normal" but a refuge.

The argument in principle is that the collective trauma engenders a natural psychological possibility of becoming attached to that charismatic leader who has undergone a similar trauma in his own life. He, unlike most people, has already been through a similar experience and learned more or less how to cope with it. Therefore, at this rare meeting point, he already knows how to project a feeling of coping effectively with the situation and, no less important—according to the followers' perception—he understands the psychological nuances of the situation out of his own personal experiences. This does not mean, of course, that this charismatic leader is gifted with what is known as "emotional intelligence." As described above, narcissists are not sensitive to others. Here, it is a question of sensitivity to a specific process, and only to this, on the part of the person with the trauma, for example, Jones's understanding of loneliness or Manson's understanding of the sense of marginality. Thus, with the changed circumstances, all this weight of emotion that feeds the flame, that creates the screen on which to project emotions, that forges the psychodynamic link between the specific leader and his followers in given circumstances, may be irrelevant in a different situation—and then the perception of him will also change and with it, naturally, his position. To clarify this further, historians explained the German people's readiness to follow Hitler by the nature of the crisis in Germany between the two world wars. First, life in Germany was characterized by existential uncertainty, severe unemployment, galloping inflation. Moreover, there was the story of the "knife in the back"—the surrender in World War I, which many Germans perceived as unnecessary and shameful. They believed that Germany should have gone on fighting and were deeply humiliated by the surrender. In this atmosphere, millions of German children grew up feeling anxiety and disappointment with a father who failed to make a living . . . and perhaps he was a soldier who had not fought bravely and was weak. These powerful emotional circumstances of a "disappointing father" over a long period could provide the ground for the growth of a Hitler, for whom a disappointing father was a basic life experience. He had a stronger and more obsessive urge than others to compensate for this private trauma. He knew how to play on all those painful notes, on the motifs of pride and security, and this resonated powerfully at that fatal and tragic time in the history of the period. Hitler, his essence, his words, and his passion, represented the compensation they so longed for. This is one explanation that speaks of unique dynamics between the leader and the collective at a meeting point where psychological homogeneity is born out of trauma.

Another explanation adds a different element to the dynamics of the meeting: the element of identification with the group, the collective, as a basis for that psychological homogeneity that motivates the collective to obey the leader. This argument, proposed by Lindholm,[41] links the theory of the French sociologist Emile Durkheim[42] with one of Freud's basic arguments.[43]

Durkheim argues that the individual receives his identity from the group, which gives him strength, and when individuals become a group, a new identity is formed—a collective identity. The group situation gives strength to the individual, as described by Durkheim: "Men are more confident because they feel themselves stronger, and they really are stronger, because forces which were languishing are now awakened in the consciousness."[44]

Lindholm connects this explanation with Freud's basic argument that identification is a primal expression of feelings toward others. Lindholm claims that just as romantic love is a form of identification, in which the boundaries of the individual are blurred and the ego of one merges with the other, the same psychological mechanism operates with regard to charisma.

In Lindholm's view, charisma is first of all a relationship, and in its extreme form it is like romantic love, where the boundaries are blurred and there is diffusion of the ego. This process occurs more intensively through identification with the group. The group can become an object with which one merges, and it in turn merges with the leader, and thus they all feel stronger. In fact, they are intoxicated with a sense of power. This is the basis for phenomena in which the individual identity is completely effaced, engendering that homogeneity (or homogamy as Aberbach calls it), which is the essential basis for the outburst of the conflagration.

Thus we see the conjunction of basic elements that causes the conflagration: the circumstances that create psychological homogeneity meeting the spark and the fuel.

FORCES THAT FAN THE FLAME OR COOL IT

The statement that the conflagration breaks out as a result of the conjunction of rare psychological forces in a meeting that is pure emotion is a general argument that describes the circumstances and the spark, but is not sufficiently precise with regard to the fuel. Are there differences between collectives with regard to their flammability? Would English people and Germans react in the same way to identical circumstances? Or are there differences in the tolerance threshold in face of impending or present crisis? Are there, perhaps, collectives in which homogamy, as described here, is less likely to occur? It is hard, of course, to give a definite answer to these questions. This kind of discussion is speculative in nature, but I will try to offer some criteria for observation and analysis of these questions.

The analytic concepts of this issue derive from Freud's general argument[45] that civilization is the factor that obstructs instinctive urges. In fact, civilization may be seen as the broad social expression of the concept of the superego at the personal level.

The superego obstructs the individual's urges, restricts his desires, channels them into conventional behaviors, and sets boundaries. Civilization fulfills this function at the level of the collective, and we can therefore argue that civilization, which is like a strong social superego, will be more effective in directing and obstructing instinctive, regressive urges that act more strongly in crisis situations.

This point of departure is the framework for the question posed above: Can we assume that there will be differences between collectives living in different cultures? In the same crisis conditions, are the internalized cultural codes likely to influence different populations differently with regard to the longing for a certain type of charismatic leader? A cultural code is a summary of a world view, a summary of a primary philosophy with a message concerning man's place in the universe and his relations with hidden forces.

The history of the development of cultural codes indicates that they first arose in the consciousness of groups of people in a given territorial location, and over the course of years became determinants of behavior. Hofstede[46] claims that cultures comprise three levels, which he perceives as modes of behavior and concrete practices, and these include symbols, heroes, and rituals. All these practices are derived from the same seed, which Hofstede defines as values, describing them as the "software of the mind." The difference between groups, nations, and organizations is, therefore, in the software that exists in people's minds, which dictates differences in the practice of their rituals, their symbols, and the figures they perceive as models for identification.

Comparative research conducted by Hofstede and his colleagues over more than thirty years (in fifty countries) found significant differences in those values that are the "application software." The differences were found in three areas:

1. The approach to authority;
2. The individual's self-concept, particularly in two dimensions: the relations between the individual and society and the individual's self-concept in terms of masculinity and femininity;
3. The ways of expressing emotions and controlling aggression.

In an attempt to trace the sources of the differences between cultures, Hofstede and his colleagues conducted statistical analyses, whose main purpose was to identify the variables that are most (statistically) significant in explaining the difference. In this analysis they found, for example, that the climate in which a certain collective developed plays an important part. The researchers explained this by the relation between climate and the principal means of livelihood: agriculture. The argument is that in warmer (more tropical) climates, there was less need for intervention in man's relations with nature. Vegetation grew, the natural conditions for growth of agricultural products were good, there was less damage from natural forces, and the main threat to existence came from rivalry with other groups of people living in the same territory. Those with the best chance of survival were groups that succeeded in organizing hierarchically, while maintaining a central authority that guarded balance and order and dependence on itself. In colder countries, the major threat to survival was from nature. In such conditions there was a greater need for active intervention in nature. In order to survive, it was necessary to find alternatives to agriculture (this explains, for example, the development of industry). In such societies, according to Hofstede, people learned to be less dependent on others; they learned that their existence required a larger degree of independence.

This is not the only explanation; there are others that concern the influences of dominant groups on those subject to them. The history of the growth of empires shows the development of patterns of cultural influence. It was found, for example, that nations under the Roman Empire adopted different values from nations ruled by other conquerors. This evidently indicates the accumulation of different sets of factors—climatic, historical, geopolitical. At all events, comparative research shows clearly that there are differences in the myths and behaviors of individuals living in different cultures.[47]

One of the more significant examples of myths influencing behavior is religion. According to Schachter,[48] man differs from other creatures in his ability to characterize himself and his ideas in tools and institutions. This ability is not deterministic, but volitional, and therefore artificial. Religion is an outstanding illustration of this idea. It is simply a primary philosophical view; but that is not enough, since abstract ideas have no influence. In order for them to have influence, they must be infused with life, with concrete reality. They need to be dramatized, imbued with cosmic drama.[49] For example, the tragedies of Prometheus and Dionysus are Greek dramatizations of the fate of helpless mankind in face of the hostile forces of nature. The tragedy of Jesus combines Greek and Jewish elements. This tragedy is more effective than the Greek tragedy because Jesus was supported by God, who promised that the world would be redeemed by this cosmic sacrifice.

Primary philosophy is summarized in a book or a myth that spreads by word of mouth and becomes sanctified in the course of time as established dogma. At the beginning of classic Greek civilization, we find two holy books, the *Iliad* and the *Odyssey*. Jewish culture is based on the Old Testament, and the New Testament is the basis of Christian culture. The ideas embodied in these books, which were dramatized in order to convey messages, shaped the respective cultures for generations. The *Iliad* and the *Odyssey* contain stories of the gods of Olympus, where the principle of fate ruled both gods and men. Fate is the basic idea of classic Greek culture. In the Chinese sacred writings, we find two elements in the universe: the passive yin and the active yang, which activate and balance each other and create constant changes in the universe and in human life. These changes are cyclical, and they became the characteristic principles of Chinese culture.

In order to understand the differences in religious outlooks and the messages they convey, we need to compare the figures of the gods. The gods of the Mayan and Aztec cultures, for example, created the world (in their drama) through their blood sacrifice. Therefore, future believers were required to contribute their blood or the blood of others in order to maintain the world. The God described in the Bible, who created the world through demarcating things peacefully and harmoniously, acted according to the laws of consciousness, and therefore this kind of divinity does not require human sacrifice. Similarly, according to the Chinese code, the two elements, yin and yang, balance each other peacefully, so that Chinese culture has no need for sacrifice at all.

These values, which are internalized through socialization in the family, in the schools, and in the general atmosphere, differ from one collective to another. Comparative studies indicate that three cultural variables that were examined by Hofstede and his colleagues are particularly relevant to the discussion of leadership: the attitude toward authority, the degree of individualism or collectivism in a society, and the degree of tolerance of ambiguity ("uncertainty avoidance" in Hofstede's words).

The attitude toward authority was examined by a special measure, defined as the power distance index (PDI). To clarify this, the table below presents some salient differences that were found between countries with large power distance (LPD) and small power distance (SPD).

The comparison of this dimension in fifty countries indicates consistency in terms of Hofstede's hypothesis that in countries nearer to the equator (tropical countries) there will be a higher degree of acceptance, perhaps even mystic acceptance, of authority. In places such as Malaysia, Panama, Guatemala, the Philippines, and the Arab countries, a higher degree of power distance was found than in countries such as Norway and Denmark.

Furthermore, these studies found consistency between the PDI and measures of individualism-collectivism. In countries with a strongly individualistic orientation, where the identity is based on the individual and his achievements, the criteria for relating are specific and universal, while in countries with a collectivist orientation, the identity is rooted in belonging to a social network such as a clan or tribe, and the criteria for relating are ascriptive and particular.

Differences in characteristics of societies with LPD and SPD

Large power distance	Small power distance
Inter-related skills, strength, and status	Skills, strength, and status not necessarily related
Power based on family, friends, and ability to use resources of strength (e.g., army or natural resources)	Power transmitted by formal appointment and expertise
Political changes are achieved through personal changes at the top (e.g., a coup d'état)	Political changes are achieved by changing the rules
Local political conflicts often lead to violence	Violence is rarely used to resolve political conflicts
Autocratic and oligarchic regimes based on collaboration with interest groups	Pluralistic regimes based on election results

Based on G. Hofstede (1997). *Cultures and Organizations: Software of the Mind* (p. 37). New York: McGraw-Hill.

Countries that received a high score in the PDI were graded low in individualism, and vice versa. In other words, a negative correlation was found between these two indexes. Countries graded high in PDI were also higher in collectivism, and those with a low degree of PDI were higher in individualism.

Another cultural index, perhaps particularly important for the discussion on the critical aspect of a situation, is the dimension of "uncertainty avoidance." This relates to the argument that there are differences between societies with regard to the degree of their inherent anxiety in the context of uncertainty. There are societies that are characterized by a higher degree of anxiety, a lower degree of tolerance of uncertainty, and these have psychological, social, and sociological implications. Such societies use various means to deal with that anxiety.

The idea that variables such as levels of anxiety merit sociological examination is not new. Back in 1897, Emile Durkheim[50] published his research on suicide and showed that the proportions of suicides in different countries remained stable over many years. He argued that the stability of these findings indicated that even such a personal act as taking one's own life is influenced by social forces that differ from one country to another.

Suicides are only one possible result of high levels of anxiety. In the 1970s, an Irish psychologist, Richard Lynn,[51] published a comparative study on anxiety and its results. The study was conducted in eighteen countries, and the statistical data were taken from the official health authorities. They covered such matters as suicide rates, alcoholism, deaths from heart disease, and the rate of chronic psychotic phenomena. These findings matched the findings of another study that was conducted by Hofstede in 1980,[52] which used a different type of data to measure anxiety levels. These two studies show clearly that the anxiety level in some cultures is higher than in others. In those countries with a high anxiety level, more steps (or more intensive steps) are taken to prevent uncertainty, which raises anxiety yet further. The table below summarizes the main differences between levels of anxiety and levels of uncertainty.

Differences in characteristics of societies with
high and low uncertainty levels

Strong uncertainty avoidance	Weak uncertainty avoidance
Uncertainty is a threat that has to be fought	Uncertainty is a normal part of life and is accepted as such
High stress level, subjective feelings of anxiety, aggressive feelings in certain circumstances can be externalized as an expression of release	Low stress level, good subjective feelings, aggressive feelings are not worth expressing
Whatever is different is a threat	What is different is interesting and arouses curiosity

Based on G. Hofstede (1997). *Cultures and Organizations: Software of the Mind* (p. 125). New York: McGraw-Hill.

As stated, societies and cultures differ in their ways of coping with uncertainty. Countries with a high level of anxiety related to uncertainty evince strong uncertainty avoidance. This is expressed in rules and laws and in public attitudes and moods. (In Germany, for example, there are laws that acquire validity when all the other laws cannot be implemented for any reason, while Britain does not even have a written constitution.) Countries that practice extensive uncertainty avoidance are more conservative, more suspicious of youth, more nationalistic, more xenophobic, more ideologically rigid, believe more in formal knowledge, and so forth.

These findings may indicate predispositions of collectives with regard to the acceptance of a hypnotic leader and the willingness to be influenced by such a leader. It may be assumed that in cultures characterized by large power distance, a more collectivist orientation, and a high level of uncertainty-related anxiety, the probable emergence and influence of a hypnotic leader is stronger than in collectives with small power distance, more individuality, and a lower level of uncertainty-related anxiety. In the latter case the psychological conditions for the emergence of that homogamy, that psychological homogeneity of the followers, which is the basis for the conflagration, are much less likely to occur. Naturally, it would be hard to prove this argument with empirical research, and it is largely deduced from retrospective analysis, but there is considerable research evidence on differences between international organizations, such as IBM, that operate in a number of countries. The evidence indicates that although these are companies with one central management (usually American) and directions and procedures based on the policy set by the central management, there is a great deal of difference between the subsidiary companies in their ongoing management, attitude to authority, staff's attitude to their work groups, and the need for clear instructions versus space for independent thinking and acting.[53] Many managers who were thought to be gifted failed because of their inability to understand the "different software" at the base of the local culture. If the research evidence shows differences in management in the context of different cultures, there is no reason to assume that these differences in "software" will not be significant in relation to leaders in crisis situations.

Thus far, the argument with regard to the major factors in the discussion. But that is not enough: There are other significant factors in the dynamics that obstruct or enhance charisma. One of the most observable is age: The younger the people, the less complex and more emotional is their judgment and perception (as we can see in their worship of folk heroes such as actors, singers, and sports stars). The saying, "Anyone who is not a socialist (that is, an idealist who wants to change the world) at twenty has no heart, and anyone who is still a socialist at forty has no brain" seems to be a somewhat cynical reflection of the effect of age. (What happened to the leaders of the flower children from the late 1960s and the radical world-changing student leaders like Daniel Cohn-Bendit?) The tendency—perhaps one should say the wish—to become impassioned, to be swept away, to fall in love with someone who radiates emotionality, often becomes less intense as people grow older. It is, apparently, not by chance that the members of charismatic leaders' sects, as well as religious repentants of various kinds, have always been young. Questions of identity, as the developmental psychologist Erikson described so well, are most pressing among young people, and hence they are more susceptible to the influence of charismatic leaders.

Another factor that spurs uninhibited behavior and increases the likelihood of such behavior appearing is anonymity. There is research evidence of this in social psychology. Phillip Zimbardo,[54] a social psychologist, believed that the loss of individuality creates conditions for throwing off restraint even to the extent of violent outbursts. In a laboratory experiment, he sought to examine whether the feeling of lack of identity makes man violent. Zimbardo brought students to the laboratory in groups of four. In order to create a sense of anonymity, he did not call them by their names, seated them in a dark room, and had them wear overalls and masks.

In another group, which served as a comparison group, the individuality of the subjects was emphasized. The researcher called them by their names, each one was asked to wear a name tag, they sat in a well-lit room, and did not wear overalls or masks. All the subjects were told that they were taking part in an experiment to examine the ability to identify with others. The researcher, so they thought, wished to examine how much their identification with others was influenced by a manipulation in the form of an electric shock given to another person. The subjects were asked to give an electric shock twenty times to a young woman whom they could see while the researcher was interviewing her. This young woman was, in fact, an actress who was collaborating with the researcher, and the subjects saw her on closed circuit TV. The whole situation was staged, and she could be seen moving her arm each time the electric shock was administered.

The results of the experiment showed that the duration of the electric shock given by the students in conditions of anonymity was double the time given when the subjects' individual identity was emphasized. Furthermore, the duration of the shock administered by the anonymous students grew stronger during the course of the experiment.

The masks in Zimbardo's experiment were real masks, such as can be found in situations outside laboratory experiments, in social

ceremonies of various kinds. We remember the infamous Ku Klux
Klan masks, which evidently allowed their wearers to behave more
violently and cruelly than they might have done if their identity
had not been hidden. However, the mask does not have to be a
physical one. It can be a metaphoric mask in many social situations:
in military units, factories, mass demonstrations, all of which operate like a collective mask. This, along with other factors, adds to the
possible emergence of hypnotic leadership.

We could describe additional factors that carry weight in analyzing how the meeting of leaders, followers, and circumstances creates fire. However, it seems to me that the variables presented
above are sufficient to create a conceptual framework for more
comprehensive discussion.

Now that we have a general conceptual framework for analysis
of these forces working to create fire, I wish to introduce the myth
effect, which is a major cultural element that determines behavior.
The most outstanding example of its effect was in Nazi Germany.
Using this example, I will attempt to demonstrate the power of cultural codes (expressed through myths) in blocking or catalyzing impulses that arise spontaneously in crisis situations. This analysis will
be done in the framework of Kurt Lewin's "field forces" concept.

THE FAUST-MEPHISTOPHELES MYTH

The German myth of Faust is the legend of a man who sells his
soul to the devil in return for having his wishes granted. This myth
(like many others) has it source in religion. To understand how it developed, we need to understand the religious sources from which it
sprang. After the Reformation period, Christianity split into three
streams: The first remained true to the Catholic Church and continued to believe that the Kingdom of Heaven was embodied in the
Church, the second adopted Calvin's theology and returned to bibli-
cal values, and the third adopted Luther's principles.

The Germans adopted Luther's theology, which, as will be described below, developed into Faustianism, resulting in an entirely
different ethical-mythological code from the other two streams.

What is Faustian folklore? The Faustian myth is the dramatized expression of Luther's theology. In order to understand this, we need to return to the description of Goethe's play about Faust. The play presents all the important motifs in the discussion of archetypes, codes, and insidious influences, as these find expression in German culture. In the prologue to the play, there is a return to archetypes. Divinity, for example, is described very differently from the way it is described in other books. God is portrayed in the play as a ridiculous old nuisance, and beside him the figure of Satan (Mephistopheles) is a much more impressive figure. Goethe's prologue portrays God as bored with the society of the good angels, Gabriel, Uriel, and others, who praise him. He prefers his mischievous son, Mephistopheles. There is no mention of Jesus in the prologue. Only the devil is given cosmic dimensions; he is the most impressive character in the new pantheon. God sends Mephistopheles to spur lazy humanity to be more active. There is no message of redemption or of improving the state of the world. God only wants his beloved son Mephistopheles to go down to the world and rouse man to stop being lazy in his work. Doctor Faust, the hero of Goethe's drama, the man who made a pact with the devil Mephistopheles, lived during the Reformation period and was an alchemist who dealt in magic. He professed to have supernatural powers. During his life, he was a marginal person of the type the Church used to suppress. Faust was tired of casuistry, of the study of philosophy and theology that did not solve his problems. He realized that he had no answer to the riddle of the world after all he had read and had learned. He did not want to remain bound by moral debates that demanded restraint of him. He refused to be restrained; he wanted to start life anew. He wanted everything! He wanted action. Goethe, through Faust, described the true meaning of Lutheran theology: the emphasis on action. The message transmitted by the Faust-Mephistopheles myth is that it is possible to achieve more than reality permits. Faust makes a pact with the devil in order to attain the highest pleasures and receive supernatural powers from him. For a moment, he is ready to ignore the fear of the devil, who will demand his soul in return for the pleasures he bestows.

This story might be dismissed as just another folk tale, but the fact is that the Faustian myth has occupied German writers and artists to an extent that is unparalleled anywhere else. There have been at least twenty adaptations of the Faustian myth in Germany alone, including musical versions.

From a historical perspective, some historians argue that the "message of the act" is the thing that was needed to unite Germany; action accompanied by power.[55] Perhaps it was not by chance that forty years after the play *Faust* was written, in 1871, Germany was united under the rule of Bismarck.

Luther's theory is hard to explain in a few words. It has no parallel in any other culture. Since Luther adopted the devil as the only present God, he relegated Jesus to the minor role of cosmic sacrifice. Outside the borders of Germany, both Protestants and Jews paid little attention to Luther's new principles and knew him mainly as the translator of the scriptures. Thus he was mistakenly viewed as the person who restored the scriptures to their greatness, while in fact he emptied them of content.

Religion is an institution that was created to satisfy man's longing for hidden powers so that he might be granted his desires. In return for every request, every pleasure, a person must pay the hidden powers. This is the source of the sacrifices that people used to make to hidden powers or gods. This religious archetype matches the way the human consciousness works. This consciousness reached the conclusion that everything has to be paid for. The various religions and cultures differ in the form of payment. Some sacrificed animals and offered up precious articles to the gods, some practiced self-castigation, and some sacrificed humans. Christianity created the cosmic "one-time" sacrifice—of Jesus—to bring about a change, after which there would be no more need for sacrifices. (In the Catholic mass, every participant is metaphorically sacrificed together with Jesus and redeemed together with him.) Luther crowned the devil, but according to the principle of payment, a person who asks for something special has to pay more. Satan, symbolizing evil, who aspires to remove every obstacle, demands of man the thing that is most important to him in return for the pleasures he grants—his soul. Luther did not develop the myth to the end. He clung to Jesus, to the idea of the cosmic sacrifice, to ensure the immortality of his soul. Although he made the devil king, he feared that he would take his soul away. All his life he struggled with this unresolved issue.

The story, which was later dramatized by Goethe and became a great myth, solved the problem of the high price. Faust, the folklore character in the drama, signed a contract with the devil but managed in the end to trick him and obtain the pleasant part of the contract without having to give his soul in return.

This story and its influence are apparently very German. The fact is that the Faustian myth was very popular in Germany and not so popular anywhere else. In England, for example, when the play *Faust* was staged, it was greeted with contempt, disgust, and revulsion.[56] The English cultural code did not support the view that a person's deeds do not stain his soul. Thus, we can conclude that without a supporting theology, a folk hero like Faust cannot become a national hero. He could not become a hero transforming the English nation because he did not suit the English theology.

This discussion may appear to be completely hypothetical and of interest only to academics who deal with archetypes, theologies, and similar abstractions that have nothing to do with the real influence of leaders. However, despite Germany's adoption of Faustianism (Nietzsche and Oswald Spengler spoke of the Faustianism of the German soul), clear-sighted Germans, even before the rise of the Third Reich, perceived the great danger threatening the whole of Europe from the German culture. The most prominent of those who foresaw this danger was Heinrich Heine, who argued fiercely that beneath the German so-called spirituality lay fierce barbarism. Heine lived most of his life in France and, perhaps, that is why he argued that he could discern the true essence of the German culture and its occupation with demonology.

Thomas Mann, in his book *Doctor Faustus*, pointed to the negative elements of Faustianism. Later, in a lecture he gave in the United States in 1945, he showed clearly and unambiguously the connecting thread between Luther, Faust, Satan, and the Third

Reich. Thus, as researcher Rivka Schechter points out, the Third Reich and Hitler's success have theological roots.[57]

To sum up, we can formulate some propositions based on the above descriptions. On the face of it, some of these propositions appear obvious, but it seems to me that people do not tend to question or reflect on their deeper meanings. Perhaps the ideas presented here will give some of the arguments a more dynamic dimension than the common clichés on leadership.

First, as the descriptions indicate, leaders need followers no less than followers need leaders. There is a tendency to forget this. In most cases, and certainly in the more extreme ones, the relationship between a leader and his followers is like that between an actor and his audience. Surprising as it may seem, many leaders need followers to strengthen their self-confidence and self-image, and sometimes even to give a basic sense of meaning to their lives. The picture that is usually portrayed is the opposite: Either the leaders one-sidedly plant confidence and hope in their followers, or their influence on their followers is described in absolute terms—the followers are described as malleable objects. This description is usually one-dimensional, one-sided, and not at all accurate.

Second, we see clearly that it is not just a matter of mutual relations but in the more extreme cases (represented by hypnotic leadership), one of highly charged emotional relationships. Not for nothing have some writers compared leader-led relations with love affairs.[58] Love can be destructive and even fatal. Moreover, as with certain love affairs, the objects of love can sometimes feel and even analyze soberly the dangers that love causes them, yet they do not find the strength to free themselves from its bonds. Love in these stages can be like strong drink to an alcoholic or drugs to an addict: The addiction leads to total dependence. But in this case, both sides are dependent because of the interaction between them.

Third, to continue the comparison with love relations, different people have different predispositions for involvement in dependency relationships. These tendencies have their source in early psychodynamics, images in the culture and the social environment, and the combination of circumstances.

Fourth, we cannot ignore the enormous power of the group, the crowd, to blur the identity of the individual, and the power of instinctive unconscious primary forces. The examples cited in this book are only a small sample of this power, and the question arises as to what comes first, the leader's influence or the growth of uniformity within the group, enabling the leader to exert influence in a way that perhaps could not be achieved in one-to-one relationships.

Fifth, the examples and analyses presented in this book explain (either explicitly or implicitly) that the process usually consists of two stages: the stage of acceptance, choice of the leader, and the stage of the leader's emotional influence, which usually occurs gradually. These stages can be distinguished, and the actual distinction between them can advance our thinking on the formation of a context-dependent model that will describe the conditions for the existence and development of hypnotic leadership. It seems that the followers and the cultural-environmental context (economic, social, military) have great weight at the stage of acceptance and choice of a leader.

In the second stage, *after* the leader has been accepted, the leader's ability for emotional expression, his ability gradually to exert influence and create legitimacy for primary emotions, carries greater weight. All the examples cited in this book demonstrate the distinction between the stages and the gradual development of emotions, development that is psychologically denied at each station along the way.

Finally, this is a complex and dynamic phenomenon that involves many factors and processes, some of which are not visible at a casual glance. Therefore, as with many social phenomena, the attempt to isolate every factor and evaluate its influence is not sufficient. Nevertheless, a careful examination of past events that demonstrate this phenomenon can help us to analyze the processes that result in what I have called "hypnotic leadership."

Some Thoughts in Conclusion

Blind faith in authority is the greatest enemy of truth.
                                                      Albert Einstein

A friend asked me a banal question. "Have you noticed that visitors usually say the most interesting or important things just when they are at the door on their way out?" I assume that this feeling is inherent in the nature of last words, at the end of an evening, of a meeting, the end of a book: It is the wish to sum up but also to leave an opening for next time.

I really do not want to sum up. In this chapter, I want to open another window and cast light on other points worth thinking about that I have not dealt with in the book up to now, or only hinted at. In my opinion, it is not possible to discuss leadership, and certainly not to sum up a book on leadership, without considering these points at least superficially. Therefore, I will present the points I consider most pertinent to the discussion in the book, noting that I believe that the images associated with leadership are changing and will change substantially in the future.

LEADERSHIP AND INFLUENCE

Numerous books and articles have dealt with the concept of power and its expression in organizations, in politics, and in various social deployments. As usually happens in academic discussions, the concept of power has acquired many different definitions and perspectives. However, I believe that if someone points a pistol at your head, no matter what the formal definition, it is perfectly clear which of you has the power. Power in its pure and simple form is, therefore, the ability to force your will on others because you control the resources, which may be threats (a gun) or something rare and needed (oil, or the most precious resource of all in modern times—knowledge).

James McGregor Burns, an eminent professor of history and political science, engaged for many years in research and writing on the leadership of some outstanding presidents of the United States (he published books on Roosevelt[1] and Kennedy,[2] and even won the Pulitzer Prize for one of the most riveting books ever written on the subject of leadership[3]). He discusses an apt example of the connection between power and leadership: Vietnam. The United States possessed all the possible resources of power: weapons, money, technological superiority. What it lacked was motivation. Burns shows with many further examples that motivation largely determines how power resources are used and with what intensity—and motivation is related above all to leadership.

A dynamic view of these concepts pictures them as relationships whose dynamics can be described in terms of influence, claiming that leadership is, above all, an influence on people's motivation. In fact, all the theoretical models of leadership deal with the characterization of influence.

I stress this point because many books, especially history books written about leaders, actually describe rulers, not leaders. We need to distinguish between leadership and rulership, as Burns emphasized. When people obey someone because he possesses formal authority, whether he is a king or a senior manager or a company commander, it is hard to tell whether they are acting out of an inner wish or out of the fear of some kind of punishment. The same applies to power (obedience at gunpoint, or alternatively, obedience to a medical expert). The effect on motivation is discerned in situations where there is no formal authority or intimidating power, for example, charging into battle following a commander or working overtime for long hours without financial reward just because of the personal influence of the one in charge. It is easy to discern this added value that is called "influence." It is often found that among certain companies in the same regiment, in the same field conditions, with the same means and identical training programs—in other words, with all the same conditions—one company surpasses all the others in achievements and motivation. This is the influence of the company commander; not his formal authority or his physical resources, but his influence—his personal leadership.

The academic definition distinguishes between agreement and response,[4] between instrumental motivation and commitment.[5] Commitment is the willingness to do things that cannot be formulated in terms of cost-benefit in the instrumental sense: to take risks and make efforts, to do things that one does not have to do when one is alone without supervision and without the influence of others. This is the space where the main discussion on leadership takes place.

LEADERSHIP AND CIRCLES OF INFLUENCE

The examples in this book (which are not intended as a sample, but simply as points of reference) have dealt with leadership in various circles of influence: in an intimate group where each member is in direct contact with the leader, in a large group where most of the followers are not so close to the leader, and leadership of an entire nation, where the leader is distant from nearly all of his followers except for a select few.

Does the distance from the leader affect the strength and nature of his influence? Can the conclusions drawn from the observation of leadership in a small or large group (for example, an organization) be applied to leadership of a nation? If an officer is an excellent leader as a company commander, does this mean he will excel as leader of an entire army? Or as a political leader? Is people's willingness to accept a leader in an organization similar to the willingness of people choosing their political leaders? And beyond the question of choice, is it the same kind of influence? The surprising fact is that these questions, which are so fundamental and relevant, have barely been discussed. And as for the question asked above, namely the distance from the leader, it is only recently that the research literature has begun to deal with it in any depth.[6]

The question of distance from the leader is highly relevant because of the followers' importance in the triangle of leader, followers, and circumstances. If leaders are largely the result of projections, attributions, and transference—in other words, the followers' perceptions—the question of distance from the leaders may be cardinal. In the language of academic research, perception of the leader may be a critical intervening variable which, in turn, is influenced by various factors. In such an equation, there is no doubt that distance may be very significant.

I recently found myself considering this question on a personal level when I happened to meet one of my old youth movement leaders whom I had not seen since childhood. This was a leader who was highly admired and gifted with all the attributes that we (his charges) could lavish on him: handsome, articulate, charming, charismatic. Describing the meeting to my close friends who had known him back in those days, I could not help saying with laughter mingled with disappointment, "I could swear that he was much taller then." To be honest, I was really disappointed that I had met him. His image from the past was much larger in my memory, perhaps larger than life. I was small and he was big, distant, and all the girls we loved (usually in secret) were in love with him. It is no wonder that we could see him as the embodiment of all our wishes. Are distant leaders the embodiment of wishes? As Nixon complained angrily after being defeated by Kennedy, "They [the electorate] see in him [in Kennedy] what they would like to be." Does distance give the followers a much broader range of projection or attribution error? In other words, can a more distant leader be less a real figure and more a subjective creation? These questions are significant in light of the many axiomatic descriptions of leadership. The main axiom is, of course, that the leader's personal example influences the followers more than anything else. Is this the case no matter what the distance? There is a great deal of evidence showing that, in the case of great distance from the leader, this view is at best simplistic and, in the historical perspective, even absurd.

Let me expand on this point a little. In a book dealing with the leadership of managers in organizations,[7] I collated material written on effective channels of influence of leaders in organizations. The effectiveness of leaders' influence in organizations was analyzed on the basis of the distinction formulated by a researcher and philosopher of management, Chris Argyris.[8] According to Argyris, two types of theories exist in organizations. One is espoused theory, which appears in the statements of managers, formal documents that express statements of intention, vision, goals, and so forth. (Part of the espoused theory often appears in publications produced by the organization for distribution to visitors or on posters hanging at the entrance and in the corridors of the organization.) The other is theory in practice. This is the theory that actually dictates the behavior of people in the organization. It can easily be identified from observations and interviews held with people who work in the organization, from the production floor upwards. In these interviews, theory in practice will be reflected by clear understanding of subjects such as: "What kind of people get promoted here?" "What should one avoid in this organization?" "What do they like here?" "What do they hate here?" Briefly, "How does one get on here?" It is amazing how quickly and completely the workers in an organization grasp the coordinates of the map by which they can steer their way in the organization. Theory in practice often differs from espoused theory, which is a mixture of slogans and declarations. Theory in practice is formed and internalized in the workers' consciousness according to the managers' actions, not their declarations. The messages that have real influence affect the way they think and lead to everyday decisions: The decision to reward a certain act conveys a message that the act is important and worthy of imitation; the decision to promote a worker transmits a message concerning the criteria for promotion, and, by the same token, ignoring an action transmits a message regarding the acceptable boundaries of action.

The literature dealing with channels of influence of leaders in organizations, in other words, channels of creating theory in practice, generally describes five main channels, all of which are the leaders' "channels of action and behavior." Their essence is:

1. Time devoted by managers. The argument is that managers' time carries a message. The employers understand that if the manager devotes a lot of time to customer service, then this subject is central and important. The mere fact of allocating manager-time to a subject transmits a clear message.

2. Consistent interest. Managers/leaders in organizations do not always find the time to devote to an aspect that they would like to promote among their staff, but if they stress its importance by revealing consistent interest, this is clearly perceived by the workers. Occasional telephone calls, remarks at meetings, casual questions on the way to the restaurant or the parking lot—all focusing repeatedly on a particular aspect—convey a clear message with regard to the importance of this aspect.

3. Setting. Leaders' acts in this category are similar to stage sets. The set carries a message. For example, the type of cars purchased for the directors are an effective message; the planning of the work area in an open space design conveys a certain message, and so on.

4. Mechanisms of reward and recognition. The employees in organizations quickly grasp what acts are mentioned at various celebrations, what acts are mentioned on the notice board, in the company bulletin, what acts are rewarded with a bonus. All these responses convey messages concerning the importance of specific organizational behaviors.

5. The managers' behavior in crisis situations. As is often described in connection with leadership, crisis situations both test and heighten leaders' influence. This is a time of sensitivity, confusion, bewilderment, and it has the effect of focusing a magnifying glass on the leaders' behavior. In organizations, the behavior of leaders in a crisis situation conveys a particularly powerful message. For example, if the manager himself takes a salary cut because of the crisis, this is usually more effective than any speech asking the employees to help by agreeing to a salary cut.

All these examples stress the importance of behavior, action, and personal example in the influence of leaders in organizations. There is a great deal of evidence of this: It is axiomatic. However, at the level of national and international leadership, where many leaders are remote from daily meetings or physical presence with their followers, the evidence is diverse and contradictory with regard to the centrality of action in influencing the followers' wishes and behaviors.

In the political-ideological sense, is there any theory or message that has influenced humanity more in the twentieth century than Marxism? Karl Marx was the ideological leader not only of millions of workers who had nothing to lose "but their chains," but also of intellectuals like Bertolt Brecht, Jean-Paul Sartre, and in fact, most of the eminent European intellectuals.

Karl Marx did not come from the working classes; moreover, he never worked as a laborer in his life and never went near a shop floor.[9] These facts are not important, in my view, but the theory of leaders influencing through personal example faces a very severe test in the case of Marx. In his writings and speeches, he was given to citing examples of workers exploited with meager pay, but even he could document no example of a worker who received no wage at all. However, in his own home, in the home of the Marxist leader, there was such a worker—Lenchen. Lenchen was the nanny given to Marx's wife, Jenny, by her mother in 1845, when Lenchen was twenty-two years old. She remained with the Marx family until she died. Elinor, Marx's daughter, called her "the kindest creature in the world to other people, and stoic towards herself all her life." She was an exceptionally diligent worker, who not only cleaned, cooked, and washed but also took care of the family budget. Marx never paid her a penny and, for a certain time, made her his mistress. She bore him a son, Freddie, who had to grow up in a foster family and was never acknowledged by Marx. And all this time, Marx was describing man's exploitation of man in an incomparable manner.

Another well-known example illustrates a shocking gap between leaders' pronouncements and their behavior. Perhaps the best known feminist, one of the founding mothers of the feminist movement, was Simone de Beauvoir. The opening words of her book *The Second Sex* (written in 1949), which became the first feminist manifesto, are: "One is not born a woman, one becomes a woman." These words became a powerful slogan. But this clear message is in complete contrast to de Beauvoir's own life with Jean-Paul Sartre. According to all her friends, Sartre treated her worse than a servant and was openly cruel to her in public, while she, in some strange and incomprehensible way, swallowed every insult—in total contrast to the messages she preached to other women throughout the world.

These are just a few of the examples one could cite, and in this context we could add John Kennedy and his words about the importance of the American family; Moshe Dayan, Franklin Delano Roosevelt, Douglas MacArthur, and many others, figures who were controversial in their private lives, who can scarcely be seen as paragons, certainly not as paragons of virtue in their daily actions and behaviors, but who nevertheless had great influence as leaders.

Is there a different psychological mechanism at work in the case of remote leaders' influence? The examples and analyses presented here (and in many other publications) suggest that this is indeed the case. This argument is definitely consistent with the contribution of Max Weber and many others in his wake, who argued that leadership is above all the followers' subjective perception. The classification of this perception into projection, transference, and attribution is a sophisticated (and important) refinement of specific psychological disciplines. From this point of view, there must be differences between near and distant leaders. The close contact with the leader limits the projective aspect because it is easier to project onto distant figures.

Evidence relating to some of the examples presented here, among others, shows that people close to the leader were not always among his greatest admirers. For example, Engels, who was at Marx's side for decades and his partner in writing his most important documents, did not at all admire the leader's character. In the view of those close to them, the leaders were people with vices and virtues, not just the personification of ideas. And this, perhaps, is the main difference.

Victor Hugo said, in another context, "Nothing is stronger than an idea whose time has come." However, being an abstract thing, an idea is not always understood. Personification of the idea makes it easier to focus projections and desires on it. Karl Marx would apparently have been consigned to oblivion had he tried to exert influence a century earlier. Furthermore, Marx did not succeed in projecting in the United States what he did in Europe. The United States did not have an "old order"—an establishment with special privileges based on ownership by tradition. There was no old order that people perceived as unjust and were motivated to destroy. The United States itself was a product of a revolution against the injustices of the old world. Its constitution was written and implemented on the basis of early experience of the evils of European regimes. So we see that the aspect of distance augments the oxygen in the metaphor of leadership as fire. Indeed, there are researchers who believe that great distance is a necessary condition for charisma. Leaders who are too accessible will never be perceived as charismatic.[10] It appears that when the leader is freed from the criteria for evaluation of leadership acts described above as channels of action and behavior, the followers no longer relate to the true figure of the leader but to what he is supposed to represent, no matter how this is explained.

The distinction made here with regard to distance in relation to leaders' acts and influence does not necessarily mean that distant leaders with repugnant behavior do not contribute to the development of human society and humanitarian thinking. In many cases, people you would not want to invite into your home have contributed enormously as humanitarian leaders.

This is not a new idea. In fact, it was aptly expressed by the German philosopher Georg Friedrich Hegel (1770–1813). History, according to Hegel, is humanity's development and progress toward a wiser and freer society and state. Hegel portrays the driving force of that development as an entity that he calls the "spirit of the world," whose main characteristic is intelligence. World history,

says Hegel, is simply the development of thought or the appearance of the spirit of the world in its various manifestations, but being intelligent inevitably entails being free and, therefore, "history
is nothing other than progress in the consciousness of freedom." This
argument is not original, of course; it has a platonic basis. However,
and here Hegel adds an interesting link that recalls Machiavelli's
ideas, a close study of history shows that people's activity stems
from their needs, desires, interests, and character. Thus, on the one
hand, there is development of intelligent ideas; on the other hand,
practical history has its source in the human desires and interests of
individual people. This contradiction can be seen in the actions of
outstanding leaders such as Alexander the Great or Julius Caesar.
Their great achievements were motivated above all by their lust for
power, but at the same time their actions helped to advance the
spirit of the world and brought human society to a more developed
stage. The leader, according to Hegelian logic, is a private person
who fulfills a social or historical need. This is Hegel's dialectic regarding the leader (the spark), the followers (the fuel), and the oxygen (the circumstances at a given point in history). The leader's
influence can only be understood through analysis of this dialectic.
"The leader," says Hegel, "is a Machiavellian leader who fulfills a
Platonic idea."[11]

MORE ABOUT THE DEVELOPMENT OF LEADERS

Churchill's assumption (at least with regard to himself) that
leadership is the result of motivation engendered by an unhappy
childhood may be an overly simplistic explanation. Therefore, I
would like to discuss this further and offer some more thoughts.
Leadership is the product of two factors: potential and motivation.
I refer to this as a mathematical product because if the value of one
of the factors is zero, then the result of the multiplication is zero,
and there is no possibility of a leader emerging. In other words, a
person with leadership potential who does not aspire to be a leader
will not develop into a leader. And vice versa: A person may desire
with all his heart to be a leader, but if he does not have the potential,

it will not come about. This argument is relevant to every outstanding human manifestation. Someone who does not have a musical
ear will never be a second Arthur Rubinstein, no matter how
strongly motivated he is, just as someone who has the potential to
be a musician but lacks motivation will clearly not realize his potential. Who has heard of Irvin Nirgihazy? He was an enormously
gifted musical prodigy who became the subject of intensive study
by the director of the psychological laboratory in Amsterdam. He
began to compose music before he was four years old, he had a
perfect ear and an excellent musical memory but, like many child
prodigies, he never fulfilled the hopes pinned on him in his
childhood. (Only 10 percent of child prodigies become virtuosi as
adults.)[12] To fulfill their potential they also need uncompromising
determination.

I stress this distinction, which is perhaps self-evident, because I
want to draw attention to two points.

A. All leaders possess both qualities: the potential to be leaders and the
   motivation to lead. In this book I have focused mainly on motivation.
   Furthermore, the leaders mentioned in this book exemplify motivation
   at a level of determination that I have called obsession. However, in reality, the range of motivation to lead is much broader and is not always
   so intense as I have described. The question of potential to lead is not
   touched on in this book because it is a puzzling question for which we
   have few answers, although there is some genetic evidence today with
   regard to other human talents, and there has recently been some progress in identifying leadership potential, both in theory and research.
B. The aspect of motivation "to compensate for childhood events," as
   many famous people have described, also contains many nuances.
   Seeking compensation does not necessarily lead to leadership, which
   brings us back to the equation of potential and motivation. For example, the urge for compensation may find artistic expression in painting,
   writing, or scientific research, which may reflect a personality with
   strong motivation and determination to express it publicly but without
   the potential (or motivation) to lead. The difference between such people and outstanding leaders is in their relationships with others, particularly in the existential meaning that the others' attitude holds for
   them. The essence of leaders' existence is, as we have seen, the feeling
   that other people give them. In the case of artists and scientists, their

psychological essence is based in another source, and their self-perception does not depend on their relationships with others. A salient example of this kind of person, which has also been analyzed in psychodynamic terms,[13] is Albert Einstein. He jealously guarded his isolation, regarding it as a basic need for his creativity. "It is highly necessary," he said, "in the kind of society we live in."[14] He also explained the fact of his being an enthusiastic violinist by his need "to be free of dependence on people." This theme appears among many creative artists. They find meaning and value in their work that others find in relationships with people. Moreover, one can rely on creative work more than on people, who are often perceived as untrustworthy.

The proof of this argument is the unchallenged and unique originality of Einstein's discoveries. His discoveries are the outcome of pure thinking, unsupported at first by an abundance of experiments or by exceptional knowledge of mathematics. His essay on relativity theory, which was published in 1905, contains no references and very little mathematics, and cites no authoritative sources. In fact, Einstein's real knowledge of mathematics was limited at that time compared with other great physicists. At the age of twenty-three, Einstein was already the person whom the world would later try to understand. Indeed, as experts on his work testify, Einstein created a new model of the universe, and for this purpose he had to cut himself off from the conventional ways of looking at things. In this sense, Einstein is an example of a person who could create new thinking on a purely theoretical basis only by severing himself from other human beings, from his previous way of thinking, and from conventional knowledge.

We know of cases in which the artist identifies entirely with his work. A representative example of this is cited by André Maurois in describing the life of Honoré de Balzac. Balzac had an insatiable hunger for love and fame. While he was still in school he used to say, "I will be famous." In his letters to a friend he wrote, "My one enormous desire is to be famous and loved."[15] He achieved both, but that did not prevent him from immersing himself in his creative work when he was already famous and revered.

The idea of creative work as a therapeutic solution has been discussed in psychological literature and even suggested intuitively by some artists. The British poet laureate, Ted Hughes, talking to a journalist about the suicide of his wife, the writer Sylvia Plath, described her "terrible urge" to write, the state of deep distress she fell into when she could not realize this urge. He inadvertently mentioned that, at a certain stage in their life together, he was inclined to think that "Sylvia was on the way to psychological recovery," because she had stopped writing, and he saw this as a sign of mental balance. Hughes remarked that if this had continued, in other words, if she had freed herself of the obsessive need to write, he would have seen it as a sign of complete recovery.

Thus, similar motivations, even at the most extreme levels, may find different channels of expression. Only in certain cases, apparently very few, will the motivation be expressed in a longing for leadership. In other cases, the inner fire that burns will find different outlets. The outlet is also determined by the other part of the equation—the potential, where the individual's basic abilities are stored: the musician's perfect ear or the writer's verbal ability.

We do not possess many findings on this subject, and developmental psychology has not dealt much with leadership. However, in the last few years there have been some theoretical studies that may further our understanding regarding the development of leaders and particularly the understanding as to why some leaders develop as "socialized charismatic leaders" and some as "personalized charismatic leaders."

Personalized charismatic leaders are characterized by the following:[16] (a) dominant and authoritarian behavior; (b) self-serving behavior and self-aggrandization; (c) exploitative behavior; (d) ignoring the rights and feelings of others, often revealing uncontrolled aggression.

Socialized charismatic leaders are characterized by (a) egalitarian behavior; (b) serving the interests of the collective, not motivated by self-interest; (c) empowerment of the followers; and (d) consideration of other people's feelings and rights, and the conventional game rules.

This is a behavioral distinction that stems from personality differences, the most important of which for our discussion are the need for power, narcissism, and Machiavellianism (placing self-interest over the interests of others, not stopping at deceit and manipulation). All these tendencies can today be diagnosed and investigated. The preliminary findings of empirical research support the argument that personalized charismatic leaders greatly exceed socialized charismatic leaders in the need for power and in narcissism and Machiavellianism.[17] It is hard to find satisfactory explanations for the sources of these differences, but some important contributions to the theory of infant development can help to further our understanding in this obscure area. The most relevant contribution to this discussion is John Bowlby's[18] theory, which is considered one of the most important in the last thirty years and contributes greatly to the understanding of the sources of human behavior in various aspects of life.

Bowlby, like most theoreticians, sees the primary interactions between the baby and his mother as a central factor in the psychological development of every individual. But, unlike most theoreticians, Bowlby sees the emotional attachment to the mother as a primary need (primary needs are those based on instinctive urges such as hunger, thirst, sex). In other words, emotional attachment to the mother, to the figure of the caregiver, is on a level with food and sleep, and just as the baby, like every other organism, will die if it is denied food, the same thing will happen to the baby, according to Bowlby, if it isolated from all ability to attach itself to some figure. This thinking of Bowlby's was deeply influenced by Darwin's theory of evolution,[19] and he supported his arguments with findings from the well-known works of Lorenz[20] and Harlow.[21] These works succeeded in showing that even in less highly developed animals than man (ducks in Lorenz's work and monkeys in Harlow's), there exist systems that motivate them to attach themselves to an available figure, regardless of its other characteristics beyond availability.

These observations helped Bowlby to formulate an approach whereby the basis for the mother-child relationship is evolutionary, and it develops, as Darwin claimed, according to the developmental needs of the species. Because the human species is at the head of the ladder of philogenetic development, it is inevitable, according to Bowlby, that man will be equipped with some unique behavioral systems that evolved out of the fact that they contributed to the preservation and improvement of the species. Because the human child exists for long months in a state of helplessness, he has to be equipped with behavioral mechanisms that will help him to develop attachment to the figure who will protect him during the time when he is exposed and vulnerable. At the same time, the caregiver (usually the mother) possesses inherent complementary behavioral mechanisms whose purpose is to protect the infant and supply his needs. If we examine typical infant behaviors, such as crying, babbling, and so forth, in this light we can see them as signals whose purpose is to generate attachment to the figure of the caregiver. The practical result of these actions is survival. All these signals are simply "attachment behaviors." In general, Bowlby distinguishes between two levels of quality of attachment: "secure attachment," which provides a sense of safety and protection, since the baby is confident in the mother's availability, and "insecure attachment" (anxiety), characterized by the infant's lack of confidence in the mother's availability in situations of distress.

Attachment theory places special emphasis on real everyday events and their influence on the baby's future development. The caregiver's ability to identify the baby's signals and respond to them with the required degree of sensitivity and availability creates in the infant what Bowlby defines as an "internal working model," which will deeply influence his emotional development. This internal model can be identified by research, and there have recently been many studies measuring the link between the internal model and various adult relationships, such as love. In point of fact, this is not a new idea. Eric Berne's popular book *Games People Play*,[22] presented the theory that certain scripts formed in early childhood guide the adult through all his future relationships, both with himself and with others. Berne, followed by Harris,[23] presented four types of scripts that develop as a result of recording—unconscious assimilation of the parents' relationships with their children.

Script 1: I'm OK, you're OK. According to this inner script, the individual has positive feelings toward himself and toward others.

This is the basic script of his essential nature and the point of departure for the way he sees life with others. This script is parallel with the "secure pattern" in Bowlby's attachment theory, and it characterizes those who internalized a positive internal model due to the constant sustaining relationship with the caregiver in infancy.

Script 2: I'm not OK, you're OK. This script represents a negative or anxious attitude toward the self, in Bowlby's terms, together with the constant thought that others are good. Such people think that others are always more capable and that they themselves are not good enough.

Script 3: I'm not OK, you're not OK. This script resembles the previous one, except that, here, the others are also negative. The negative attitude is toward themselves and toward all those around them. As Harris claims, in extreme pathological cases, both scripts of "I'm not OK" are liable to lead the subject to suicide. The concepts parallel to this script in attachment theory are the anxious/ambivalent pattern. In other words, these are people whose caregivers in infancy were not consistent, not available, and not giving and did not provide them with a sense of security that they could internalize, and therefore anxiety is a central characteristic in their self-concept and their attitude toward others.[24]

Script 4: I'm OK, you're not OK. According to this inner script, the person always relates to himself positively and sees others in a negative light. In extreme cases, these people are liable to lack any real feeling toward others and to be pathologically absorbed in themselves and their self-aggrandizement. The parallel pattern to this script in attachment theory is the avoidance pattern. In other words, these are individuals whose needs and signals were largely ignored or treated insensitively in their infancy.

In recent years there has been a great deal of research on the link between internal patterns formed in infancy and relationships in adulthood. For example, a well-known study by Hazan and Shaver[25] found links between the patterns of attachment formed in infancy (as measured by various self-report questionnaires) and the quality of an individual's romantic relations. The secure pattern revealed greater ability for intimacy and giving than other patterns.

If we assume that there is a link between patterns of development in infancy and relationships in adulthood (and even show this link in empirical research), there is no reason to avoid making similar assumptions regarding leadership, because the phenomenon of leadership is simply a specific type of relationship. Therefore, the logic that underlies the argument of the internal script, the internal model that determines the nature of one's relationships with others, is as relevant to leadership as it is to love relations between couples or between parents and children.

The link between leadership potential, motivation, and the direction of leadership (personalized charismatic or socialized charismatic leadership), can be broadly formulated as follows: People who are overanxious, who do not have sufficient ego strength, cannot be in leadership positions. In Bowlby's theoretical terms, the population from which leaders may spring is one characterized by a secure pattern of attachment or an avoidance pattern. Only these have the necessary potential of ego strength. This is a necessary, though not a sufficient, condition for leadership. To become a leader, one has to want it very much; the strength of the motivation to become a leader is determined by the compensation principle. The direction of the leadership, socialized or personalized, is determined by the type of deprivation for which the leadership will compensate. Thus, we have a set of concepts relating to leadership potential and motivation, and to the direction of the leader's development. Out of this conceptual system we can formulate some distinctions that have already been partly researched.[26] For example, leaders with a secure attachment pattern will be of the socialized type (because their attitude toward themselves and toward others is positive), and it has been found that their leadership contains giving, parental elements and a pronounced social orientation. This pattern of leadership suits people like Nelson Mandela, Mahatma Gandhi, and David Ben-Gurion. It is doubtful whether this population can produce leaders of the personalized charismatic type because that type of leader can only grow out of the population with an avoidance attachment pattern. I want to make it clear that this argument does not suggest that all leaders who can be characterized as having an avoidance pattern will be personalized charismatic leaders. However, leaders of that type will come from this population because they relate positively to themselves and negatively to others. In extreme cases, their attitude toward themselves is full of self-aggrandizement while their attitude toward others is marked by manipulation and deceit (characteristics of those who do not respect others). Clearly they will reveal behavior patterns similar to those of some of the leaders who were discussed in this book.

SOME FURTHER REFLECTIONS

A friend told me not long ago that he had acquired his education as an electronics engineer at one of the best schools in the world, but his work as director-general of a company for several years had caused him to stop being an electronics engineer. "I've lost my profession," he said dryly, "only a few years have passed and I don't understand half of what the young engineers say." Indeed, anyone who is familiar with hi-tech industries knows that the changes in these fields are so rapid and so drastic that it becomes impossible to understand their psychological significance.

Sociologist Alvin Toffler describes[27] the vast changes taking place in the period that he calls the "third wave." This wave began in the 1960s and, historically, followed the first wave, which was agricultural. The second wave was based on the principle of standardization, and was characterized, for example, by labor-intensive industries such as automobile production and various kinds of metal works. (Charlie Chaplin's famous film *Modern Times* is a striking portrayal of the principles that characterized the second wave.) Toffler argues that one of the outstanding features of this wave is the huge psychological gap between the changes occurring in knowledge, technology, and work organization and people's psychological ability to absorb the meanings of these changes.

It seems that we tend to ignore, and perhaps even deny, the gap between the objective change and its psychological significance. We do not tend to think about this in everyday life, yet we are often amazed when we discover it. Almost every parent experiences this from time to time when his children ask him questions that he is unable to answer. Almost every child senses that his parents, no matter how advanced they are, "think differently." There is evidence of such gaps in every area, in every occupation, in every aspect.

Changes are occurring, as described by Toffler and others, not only in professional and technological fields and knowledge. Processes such as globalization (the world becoming a "small global village"), media exposure, changes in business hierarchies, changes in the power structure (knowledge as a power resource much more important than traditional resources such as oil or gold)—all these changes, which are always (rightly) described as dramatic, generate changes in forms of thinking, work organization, lifestyle, status structure, and self-image. In fact, every aspect that can be envisioned has changed radically in the last thirty years, including social structures that were considered unquestioned, such as the family.

Despite the fact that all this is known, apparently it is hard to understand the "big picture" and particularly hard to comprehend its full significance. This is almost certainly connected with the difficulties in relating to phenomena that are too large or too complex.[28] The salient example of this is the way many people relate to the Holocaust. Thousands of people can identify with the story of one family, of one child, but it is extremely difficult to comprehend the Holocaust in terms of six million human beings. The event was too vast and, therefore, beyond real understanding. It seems to me that, although it is incomparably different from the Holocaust, the revolution taking place today, which Toffler calls the third wave, is too big and too complex, and only now and again do we discover certain partial aspects of the vast changes.

I mention these thoughts because they arose in the context of the discussion on leadership, which is the subject of this book. Simply put, the question is: If every imaginable aspect has changed so dramatically, is it not possible that changes have taken place in the attitude towards leaders and leadership as a phenomenon?

Anyone who travels in the world and marvels at monuments such as the Great Wall of China or the magnificent palaces built by King Herod understands that these vast enterprises were carried out by a decree ordering thousands of people to work day and night, falling sick and dying unobserved, on a horrifying scale according to the historical evidence. It is hard to imagine that a leader, no matter how revered, would dare today, in the free world, to build a huge castle for his mistress like the French kings did in the Loire Valley.

These examples serve to emphasize the point that leadership may have changed radically along with many other aspects of life. The followers have become a much more central element, perhaps *the* central component in leadership in every social area where leadership can develop. This is the direction in which the rhetoric of leadership is developing. This direction, which seems quite clear to me, at least in the free democratic world, leads one to reflect on the question as to whether this development (namely the development of democratic regimes with a high level of education, advanced technology, unprecedented availability of knowledge to society at large—via the Internet, for example, and equal opportunities, at least in the formal sense) does not, in fact, weaken the forces that lead to the emergence of personalized charismatic leaders. Undoubtedly this is the stated wish of those, such as Jefferson, who formulate democratic constitutions. The system of checks and balances and separation of powers in the American constitution was designed to ensure that no leader would become overpowerful. But it is precisely in the twentieth century, the period following the "springtime of nations," the era of great democracy, that charisma has become a central issue far more than in the past.

Modernity, as analyzed by Lindholm,[29] can create two conflicting trends. On the one hand, secularism, individualism, weakening of the family, urbanization, alienation and loneliness, all of which have grown stronger in modern society, can serve as very concentrated fuel and oxygen for the growth of charismatic leaders, who are perhaps a substitute for the sense of belonging and merging that was given by the family, religion, and the village in the premodern era. On the other hand, modern life has created other substitutes for the inherent longing to which charisma is one of the answers. The outstanding and most mythological substitute in the western context, a substitute that Lasch[30] defines as the most out-standing form of substitute for charisma, is romantic love. Kernberg expresses this idea very aptly in the argument that loneli-ness is the basis both for love and for charisma.[31] Indeed, the vast quantity of poems, songs, stories, and movies about love testifies more than anything to the function that love fills in the broad psy-chological context, which is also relevant to the discussion on lead-ership. Surrender to the loved one (as to the leader) is regarded as a noble expression, so that the loss of identity became a prize rather than a price.

From another angle, this need to be "part of something" can find its expression in new channels that only modern life provides, such as work, or occupation with a career that is not only a form of liveli-hood but a vehicle for expression and belonging, or by joining what Lindholm calls the "new religions"—community frameworks or movements such as scientology.

Another type of charismatic relationship, which is symptomatic of modern life, exists in psychotherapy. In Lindholm's view, thera-peutic relationships are charismatic, but falling in love with the therapist, which is so common, becomes a healing experience pro-vided that boundaries are maintained. The primary dependence on the therapist evolves into the growth of autonomous forces. The re-lationship with the charismatic leader does not undergo this trans-formation because the leader, unlike the therapist, consciously or unconsciously wants the dependence to continue, and, as de-scribed, this dependence is mutual. All this raises the question of the leader's responsibility. It is the responsibility of the therapist not to foster dependence, and the leader should be aware of the same responsibility. Furthermore, in view of the major part played by the followers today, society needs to be more aware of the dan-gerous possibilities and should create mechanisms to reduce the in-herent dangers.

A Jerusalem author, Shulamit Har-Even, described these sub-jects in a fascinating article dealing with various models of leader-ship.[32] The first thing that gets lost in relations with charismatic leaders are facts. A situation arises whereby people have no desire to see reality with a critical eye. They are in such great need of "the joyful symbiosis with the leader," in Har-Even's words, that they can be led to believe anything regardless of the facts. "Napoleon is an example of this argument. Napoleon, who was loved by his soldiers, spent as little time as possible with the forces, and visited them only with a scented handkerchief held to his nose. Thus, this family scene, this symbiosis, like every symbiosis, does not take the facts into account."[33]

Unlike the irresponsible, theatrical, charismatic figure who plays a game that revolves around him, there are three types of leaders who represent an overridingly responsible approach: the leader who derives his authority from the law and the constitution, the leader who is a role model, and the leader who is a facilitator. Har-Even describes the differences between leaders as follows. The charismatic leader will say, "I will be good to the nation" and win applause. The authoritative leader will say, "There are rules, there are laws, we will act according to them (or create them)." The role model will say, "Follow me, I have knowledge and personal experience," while the facilitator will say, "Let's sit together and I'll try to persuade you." Because this model does not say, "Run after me," he has no chance of winning applause in the city squares, but this model requires thinking and maturity from all sides.

This book hints at the conditions conducive to the emergence of each type of leadership: distance, crisis, age, and anonymity. All of these conditions have impact, but it may be possible to create better socialization for followers, particularly in the more formative periods, and then the volume of the applause will not be the exclusive criterion for the quality of leadership.

Glossary

Anxiety—A diffuse state of being uneasy or worried about what may happen. In psychological terms, it is defined as the response to some factor, either in the environment or in the self. Psychoanalysis is mainly concerned with the latter.

Borderline personality disorder—A borderline case is someone who is on the border between neurosis (mental disorder that is not a disease of the nervous system and does not necessarily damage the ability for reality testing) and psychosis (mental disorder that usually includes failure in reality testing).

Defense mechanism—A general designation for all the techniques that are used by an individual to protect the ego from tension, unbearable conflicts, and so on. Some of the best known defense mechanisms are projection, denial, and repression (see separate definitions below).

Denial—A mechanism by which either (a) some painful experience is denied or (b) some impulse or aspect of the self is denied.

Gestalt—An integrated whole that should be observed or studied as such and loses its original meaning when divided into parts; from the German word meaning "form."

Individuation—The process in the infant's development of becoming an individual or of becoming aware that one is an individual. The term includes the idea of becoming aware that one is separate and different from others.

Introjection—The process by which the functions of an external object are taken over by its mental representation, whereby the relationship with an object "out there" is replaced by one with an imagined object "inside." The resulting mental structure is variously called an "introject," an introjected object or an internal object. Introjection is preceded by a process called internalization.

Mirroring—A process whereby, according to Winnicott, the infant finds itself reflected in its mother face.

Narcissism—Forms of self-love. The classical theory distinguishes between primary narcissism, the love of self that precedes loving others, and secondary narcissism, which is usually a defense mechanism or an attitude. Usually it refers to the tendency to use oneself as the point of reference around which experience is organized.

Narcissistic personality disorder—Diagnostic category. It embraces persons who have suffered intense injuries to self-esteem in early life, who have compensated for this by developing a grandiose conception of themselves, and who respond to attacks on their inflated self-image with rage.

Paranoia—A functional psychosis characterized by delusions of grandeur and persecution, but without intellectual deterioration. In classic cases of paranoia, the delusions are organized into a coherent, internally consistent delusional system on which the individual is prepared to act.

Paranoid anxiety—Dread of being attacked by "bad objects," either internal, projected internal, or external. Usually it refers to anxiety inferred to be the result of the individual's projecting his own denied self-destructive impulses on to external objects.

Power distance—The extent to which the less powerful members of institutions and organizations within a country expect and accept that power is distributed unequally. This is one of the dimensions of national cultures.

Power distance index (PDI)—A measure of the degree of power distance in a country's culture.

Projection—Its use in psychology refers to "viewing a mental image as objective reality." Two submeanings can be distinguished: (a) general misinterpretation of mental activity as events occurring to one, as in dreams and hallucinations, and (b) the process by which specific impulses, wishes, aspects of the self, or internal objects are imagined as being located in some object external to oneself. Projection of aspects of oneself is preceded by denial; that is, one denies that one feels such and such an emotion, has such and such a wish, but asserts that someone else does. Projection of internal objects consists in attributing to someone in one's environment feelings toward oneself that derive historically from some past external object that one has introjected, for example, imagining that X loves one the way one imagined Y did in the past. Because introjected objects may themselves be the depositories of projection, projection of internal objects may lead to endowing the recipient with aspects not only of one's past object but also one's past self.

Regression—In general, reversion to an earlier state or mode of functioning. The theory of regression presupposes that generally infantile stages of development have not been entirely outgrown, so that the earlier patterns of behavior remain available as alternative modes of functioning.

Repression—The process (defense mechanism) by which an unacceptable impulse or idea is rendered unconscious.

Superego—The part of the ego in which self—observation, self-criticism, and other reflective activities develop. The part of the ego where parental introjects are located is the superego.

Transference—The process whereby someone displaces on to another (in the original theory formulated by Freud, it was the analyst) feelings, ideas, and so on, which derive from previous figures in his life. He relates to the other person as though he were some former object in his life, or projects onto this person object-representation acquired by earlier introjections.

Trauma—In general medicine, structural damage to the body caused by the impact of some object or substance. In psychology, any totally unexpected experience that the subject is unable to assimilate. The immediate response to a psychological trauma is shock. The later effects are either spontaneous recovery (which is analogous to spontaneous healing of physical trauma) or the development of traumatic neurosis.

Uncertainty avoidance—The extent to which the members of a culture feel threatened by uncertain or unknown situations. This is one of the dimensions of national culture.

Uncertainty avoidance index (UAI)—A measure of the degree of uncertainty avoidance in a country's culture (from weak to strong).

Notes

INTRODUCTION

1. J. Reston, *Our Father Who Art in Hell* (New York: Times Books, 1981).

2. Ibid., 229.

3. N. Gallagher, "Jonestown: The Survivors' Story," *Time Magazine*, 18 November 1979, 124–136.

4. R. Schachter, *The Theological Roots of the Third Reich* (Tel Aviv: Ministry of Defense Publications, 1990). (In Hebrew)

5. J. Mason, *Closing the Account with Psychoanalysis* (Tel Aviv: Zemora Bitan, 1995). (In Hebrew)

6. S. Freud, *Moses and Monotheism. Standard Edition of the Complete Psychological Works of Sigmund Freud*, vol. 18 (London: Hogarth Press, 1939), 109–110.

7. M.F.R. Kets de Vries, *Prisoners of Leadership* (New York: John Wiley & Sons, 1989).

8. B. Shamir, "The Charismatic Relationship: Alternative Explanations and Predictions," *Leadership Quarterly* 2 (2): 81–104 (1991).

9. C. Rycroft, *Dictionary of Psychoanalysis* (London: Penguin Books, 1995).

10. C. Lindholm, *Charisma* (London: Blackwell, 1990).

11. J.O. Hertzber, "Crises and Dictatorships." *American Sociological Review* 5 (1940): 157–160.

12. R.H. Heifetz, *Leadership Without Easy Answers* (Cambridge, Mass.: Harvard University, 1994).

13. P.G. Zimbardo, "The Human Choice: Individuation, Reason and Order versus Deindividuation, Impulse and Chaos," in N.J. Arnold and D. Levine, *Nebraska Symposium on Motivation* (Lincoln, Nebraska: University of Nebraska Press, 1960).

14. D. Aberbach, "Charisma and Attachment Theory: A Cross-Disciplinary Interpretation," *International Journal of Psychoanalysis* 76 (1995): 845–855.

15. E. Fromm, *Escape from Freedom* (New York: Rinehart, 1941).

16. G. Hofstede, *Cultures and Organizations: The Software of the Mind* (New York: McGraw-Hill, 1997).

17. J.M. Howell, "Two Faces of Charisma: Socialized and Personalized Leadership in Organizations," in J.A. Conger and K.N. Kanungo (eds.) *Charismatic Leadership: The Elusive Factor in Organizational Effectiveness* (San Francisco: Jossey Bass, 1988).

CHAPTER 1: THE SPARK—HYPNOTIC LEADERS

1. R. Emmons, *Manson in His Own Words* (New York: Grove Press, 1985), 24.

2. "I Am Charles Manson" (in Hebrew), interview with Manson, *Ma'ariv*, 14 March 1997.

3. Emmons, *Manson in His Own Words*, 101.

4. T. Watson, *Will You Die for Me?* (New Jersey, Old Tappan: Fleming H. Revell, 1978), 61.

5. Ibid., 72.

6. Ibid., 61.

7. "I Am Charles Manson," 19.

8. Emmons, *Manson in His Own Words*, 14.

9. Watson, *Will You Die for Me?*, 53.

10. Emmons, *Manson in His Own Words*, 183.

11. E. Sanders, *The Family* (New York: Dutton, 1971), 129.

12. Emmons, *Manson in His Own Words*, 199.

13. T. Reiterman, and J. Jacobs, *Raven: The Untold Story of the Reverend Jim Jones and His People* (New York: Button, 1982), 15–17.

14. Ibid., 100.

15. Reston, *Our Father*, 263.

16. Reiterman and Jacobs, *Raven*, 451.

17. R. Moore, *The Jonestown Letters: Correspondence of the Moore Family, 1970–1985* (Lewistown, Minn.: Edwin Mellen Press, 1986).

18. N. Bromberg and V.V. Small, *Hitler's Psychopathology* (New York: International University Press, 1984), 20.

19. Ibid., 266.

20. Ibid.

21. J. Fest, *Hitler* (New York: Harcourt Brace, 1974).

22. H.F. Harlow, *Learning to Love* (San Francisco: Albion, 1971).

23. H.F. Harlow and M.K. Harlow, "Social Deprivation in Monkeys" *Scientific American* 267 (1962): 237–246.

24. R.H. Spitz, "Hospitalism: An Inquiry into the Genesis of Psychiatric Conditions in Early Childhood," *Psychoanalytical Studies of Children* 1 (1945): 53–74.

25. S. Wolff, *Children under Stress* (London: Allen Lane, 1969).

26. M. Rutter, *Children of Sick Parents* (Oxford: Oxford University Press, 1966).

27. N.F. Dixon, *Our Own Worst Enemy* (London: Jonathan Cape, 1987).

28. A.L. George and G.L. George, *Woodrow Wilson and Colonel House: A Personality Study* (New York: Macmillan, 1956).

29. M. Pines, "Reflections on Mirroring," *International Review of Psychoanalysis* 11 (1981): 27–42.

30. J.M. Burns, *Leadership* (New York: Harper & Row, 1975).

31. S. Ferenczi, "Bridge Symbolism and the Don Juan Legend," in *Further Contributions to the Theory and Technique of Psychoanalysis* (New York: Basic Books, 1952), 356–358.

32. D.W. Winnicott, *Playing and Reality* (London: Routledge, 1971).

33. R.B. Romanyshyn, *Psychological Life from Science to Metaphor* (Stony Stratford: The Open University Press, 1982).

34. H. Kohut, *The Analysis of the Self* (New York: Basic Books, 1971).

35. H. Lichtenstein, "The Role of Narcissism in the Emergence of Primary Identity," *International Journal of Psychoanalysis* 45 (1964): 49–56.

36. Pines, "Reflections on Mirroring," 45.

37. M. Mahler and M. Fewer, "Certain Aspects of Separation Individuation Phase," *Psychoanalytic Quarterly* 22 (1963): 1–14.

38. A. Zaleznik, "Managers and Leaders: Are They Different?" *Harvard Business Review*, March–April, 1992, 126–133.

39. Burns, *Leadership*, 46.

40. Ibid.

41. Watson, *Will You Die for Me?*, 21.

42. Burns, *Leadership*, 46.

43. Dixon, *Our Own Worst Enemy*.

44. J. Gardner, *Leading Minds: An Anatomy of Leadership* (New York: Basic Books, 1995), 33.

45. I. Or-Bach, *Hidden Worlds* (Tel Aviv: Shocken, 1992). (In Hebrew)

46. M. Choisy, "Le complex de Phoeton," *Psyche* 48 (1950).

47. N.F. Dixon, *On the Psychology of Military Incompetence* (London: Jonathan Cape, 1976).

48. Dixon, *Our Own Worst Enemy*, 59.

49. Zaleznik, *Managers and Leaders*, 126–133.

50. L. Iremonger, *The Fiery Chariot* (London: Secker & Warburg, 1970).

51. George and George, *Woodrow Wilson and Colonel House*, 44.

52. Howell, "Two Faces of Charisma," 17.

53. Kohut, *The Analysis of the Self*, 50.

54. American Psychiatric Association, *Diagnostic and Statistical Manual of Mental Disorders*, 4th ed. (Washington, D.C.: American Psychiatric Press, 1984).

55. S. Freud, "On Narcissism: An Introduction," in A. Morrison (ed.) *Essential Papers on Narcissism* (New York: New York University, 1986).

56. O. Kernberg, *Borderline Condition and Pathological Narcissism* (New York: Jason Aronson, 1975).

57. F. Fromm-Reichman, "Loneliness," *Psychiatry* 22 (1959): 1–13.

58. I. Segal, "Phenomenological Analysis of the Loneliness Experience and Its Connection to Motivation and Intimacy" (masters's thesis, Bar-Ilan University, Israel, 1988). (In Hebrew)

59. N. Schreck, ed., *The Manson File* (New York: Amok Press, 1988).

60. S. Freud, *The Life and Works of Edgar Allen Poe: A Psychoanalytic Interpretation. Standard Edition* (London: Hogarth Press, 1964), 22, 254. (Original works published in 1933)

61. D.P. McAdams, "Biography, Narrative and Lives," in D. McAdams and R. Ochberg, *Psychobiography and Life Narratives* (Durham, N.C.: Duke University Press, 1988), 1–18.

62. J.E. Mack, *A Prince of Our Disorder* (Boston: Little Brown & Company, 1976).

63. H. Lasswell, *Psychopathology and Politics* (Chicago: University of Chicago Press, 1930).

64. George and George, *Woodrow Wilson and Colonel House*, 44.

65. E.H. Erikson, *Young Man Luther: A Study in Psychoanalysis and History* (New York: Norton, 1959).

66. E.H. Erikson, *Gandhi's Truth: On the Origins of Militant Non Violence* (New York: Norton, 1969).

CHAPTER 2: THE FUEL—HYPNOTIZED FOLLOWERS

1. J. Kozinski, *Being There* (New York: Bantam Books, 1972), 33–34.

2. S. Freud, An outline of psychoanalysis. *Standard Edition of the Complete Works of Sigmund Freud* (London: Hogarth Press, 1964), 174.

3. Freud, *The Life and Works of Edgar Allen Poe*, 6.

4. Kets de Vries, *Prisoners of Leadership*, 7.

5. J.M. Post, "Narcissism and the Charismatic Leader-Follower Relationship," *Political Psychology* 7 (4), (1986): 675–688.

6. Shamir, *The Charismatic Relationship*, 8.

7. R. Darnton, *Mesmerism and the End of the Enlightenment in France* (New York: Schocken, 1968).

8. G. Le Bon, *The Crowd: A Study of the Popular Mind* (London: Ernst Benn, 1952).

9. G. Tarde, *The Laws of Imitation* (New York: Henry Holt & Co., 1903), 77.

10. L. Ross, T.M. Amabile, and J.L. Steinmatz, "Social Roles, Social Control and Biases in Social Perception Processes," *Journal of Personality and Social Psychology* 35 (1977): 485–494.

11. J.H. Baroph and R.O. Thein, "Individual Construct Accessibility, Person Memory and the Recall Judgement Link: The Case of Information Overload," *Journal of Personality and Social Psychology* 22 (1985): 293–311.

12. J.A. Conger and R.N. Kanungo, "Behavioral Dimensions of Charismatic Leadership, in J.A. Conger and R.N. Kanungo (eds.) *Charismatic Leadership* (San Francisco: Jossey-Bass, 1988), 78–97.

13. B. Shamir, R.S. House, and M.B. Arthur, "The Motivational Effects of Charismatic Leadership: A Self Concept Based Theory," *Organization Science* 4 (1993): 577–593.

14. S. Stryker, *Symbolic Interactionism: A Social Structural Version* (Menlo Park, Calif.: Benjamin Cummings, 1980).

15. R.G. Lord, "An Information Processing Approach to Social Perception, Leadership Perceptions and Behavioral Measurement in Organizational Settings," *Research in Organizational Behavior* 7 (1985): 87–128.

CHAPTER 3: THE FIRE—LEADERS, FOLLOWERS, AND CIRCUMSTANCES

1. K. Klein and R. House, "On Fire: Charismatic Leadership and Levels of Analysis," *Leadership Quarterly* 6 (2) (1995): 183–198.

2. T. Carlyle, *On Heroes, Hero-Worship and the Heroic in History* (written in 1841). (Boston: Houghton Mifflin, 1907).

3. L.M. Terman, "A Preliminary Study of the Psychology of Leadership." In C.A. Gibb *Leadership* (Harmondsworth, Middlesex: Penguin Books, 1969), 58–95.

4. R.M. Stogdill, "Personal Factors Associated with Leadership: A Survey of the Literature." In C.A. Gibb, ibid.

5. R.M. Stogdill, *Handbook of Leadership Research. Survey of Theory and Research* (Riverside, New Jersey: Free Press, 1974).

6. M. Levi, *Marxism* (Aldershot, Hants: Elgar, 1991).

7. K. Marx and F. Engels, *Selected Writings*, Vol. 1 (Tel Aviv: Merhavia, 1955), 167. (In Hebrew)

8. H.J. Leavitt, "Some Effects of Certain Communication Patterns on Group Performance," *Journal of Abnormal and Social Psychology* 46 (1955): 38–50.

9. S.N. Eisenstadt, ed., *Max Weber: On Charisma and Institution Building* (Chicago: University of Chicago Press, 1968).

10. E.P. Hollander, "Legitimacy, Power and Influence: A Perspective on Relational Features of Leadership," in M.M. Chemers and R. Aymon (eds.) *Leadership Theory and Research: Perspectives and Directions* (San Diego, Calif.: Academic Press, 1993).

11. F.E. Fiedler, *A Contingency Theory of Leadership Effectiveness* (New York: McGraw-Hill, 1967).

12. W.J. Reddin, "The 3–D Management Style Theory," *Training and Development Journal* (April 8–17, 1967).

13. V.H. Vroom and P.W. Yetton, *Leadership and Decision Making* (Pittsburgh: University of Pittsburgh Press, 1973).

14. Burns, *Leadership*, 46.

15. B.M. Bass, *Leadership and Performance Beyond Expectations* (New York: Free Press, 1985).

16. Heifetz, *Leadership Without Easy Answers*, 12.

17. C. Lindholm, *Charisma* (London: Blackwell, 1990).

18. Kets de Vries, *Prisoners of Leadership*, 7.

19. Lindholm, *Charisma*, 114.

20. E. Schein, I. Schnier, and C.H. Barker, *Coercive Persuasion: A Socio-Psychological Analysis of the "Brainwashing" of American Civilian Prisoners by the Chinese Communists* (New York: Norton & Company, 1961).

21. E. Hunter, *Brainwashing in Red China* (New York: Vanguard Press. 1951).

22. R.J. Lifton, " 'Thought Reform' of Western Civilians in Chinese Communist Prisons," *Psychiatry* 19 (1956): 173–195.

23. R.J. Lifton, *Thought Reform and the Psychology of Totalism* (New York: Norton, 1961).

24. Ibid., 435.

25. A. Ludwig, "Altered States of Consciousness," in C. Tart (ed.) *Altered States of Consciousness* (New York: Doubleday, 1972).

26. Ibid., 16.

27. K. Lewin, "Frontiers in Group Dynamics: Concept, Method, and Reality in Social Science," *Human Relations* (1947): 15–42.

28. J.A.M. Meerloo, *The Rape of the Mind. The Psychology of Thought Control, Menticide and Brainwashing* (Cleveland: World Publishing Company, 1956).

29. J.C. Moloney, "Psychic Self Abandon and Extortion of Confession," *International Journal of Psychoanalysis* 36 (1955): 53–60.

30. Ibid.

31. A.D. Biderman, "Social-Psychological Needs and 'Involuntary' Behaviors as Illustrated by Compliance and Interrogation," *Sociometry* 23 (1960): 120–147.

32. I. Festinger, *A Theory of Cognitive Dissonance* (Evanston, Ill.: Row, Peterson & Co, 1957).

33. M. Popper, "Leadership in Military Combat Units and Business Organizations: A Comparative Psychological Analysis," *Journal of Managerial Psychology* 11 (1966): 4–15.

34. K. Lang and G.E. Lang, *Collective Dynamics* (New York: Crowell, 1961), 137.

35. J.L. Freedman and S.C. Fraser, "Compliance Without Pressure: The Foot in the Door Technique," *Journal of Personality and Social Psychology* 4 (1996): 195–202.

36. S.E. Asch, "Effects of Group Pressure upon the Modification and Distortion of Judgement," in H. Guetzkow (ed.) *Groups, Leadership and Men* (Pittsburgh: Cambridge Press, 1951).

37. R.M. Kanter, "Commitment and Social Organization: A Study of Commitment Mechanism in Utopian Communities," *American Sociological Review* 33 (1965): 499–517.

38. Heifetz, *Leadership Without Easy Answers* 12.

39. M. Schlesinger, Jr., *The Coming of the New Deal* (Boston: Houghton Mifflin, 1958), 1–2.

40. Aberbach, *Charisma and Attachment Theory*, 845–846.

41. Lindholm, *Charisma*, 114.

42. E. Durkheim, "The Dualism of Human Nature and Its Social Conditions," in R. Bellan (ed.) *Emile Durkheim on Morality and Society* (Chicago: University of Chicago Press, 1973).

43. S. Freud, *Civilization and Its Discontents* (translated and edited by James Strachey) (New York: Norton, 1961).

44. E. Durkheim, *The Elementary Forms of the Religious Life* (New York: The Free Press, 1961), 387.

45. Freud, *Civilization and Its Discontents*, 44–45.

46. Hofstede, *Cultures and Organizations*, 16.

47. Ibid.

48. Schachter, *The Theological Roots of the Third Reich*, 4.

49. Ibid.

50. E. Durkheim, *Suicide* (New York: The Free Press, 1966).

51. R. Lynn, in G. Hofstede. *Cultures and Organizations* (New York: McGraw-Hill, 1997), 114.

52. G. Hofstede, *Culture's Consequences: International Differences in Work Related Values* (Beverly Hills, Calif.: Sage Publications, 1980), 108–110, 193–195.

53. Ibid.

54. Zimbardo, "The Human Choice," 13.

55. Schachter, *The Theological Roots of the Third Reich*, 145.

56. Ibid.

57. Ibid.

58. C. Lindholm, "Lovers and Leaders," *Social Science Information* 16 (1988): 3–45.

SOME THOUGHTS IN CONCLUSION

1. J.M. Burns, *Roosevelt* (New York: Harcourt Brace, 1956).

2. J.M. Burns, *Edward Kennedy and the Camelot Legacy* (New York: Norton, 1976).

3. Burns, *Roosevelt*, 46.

4. A. Etzioni, *A Comparative Analysis of Complex Organizations* (New York: The Free Press, 1975).

5. Popper, "Leadership in Militarty Combat Units," 130.

6. B. Shamir, "Social Distance and Charisma; Theoretical Notes and Exploratory Study." *Leadership Quarterly* 1 (1995): 19–48.

7. M. Popper, *On Managers as Leaders* (Tel Aviv: Tel Aviv University Press, 1994). (In Hebrew)

8. C. Argyris, *Learning and Action: Individual and Organizational* (San Francisco: Jossey Bass, 1982).

9. P. Johnson, *Intellectuals* (New York: Harper & Row, 1988).

10. P. Katz, *Public Opinion and Propaganda* (New York: Holt, Rinehart & Winston, 1964).

11. F. Hegel, *Faith and Knowledge* (New York: State University of New York, 1977).

12. A. Storr, *The Dynamics of Creation* (London: Secker & Warburg, 1972).

13. Ibid.

14. Ibid.

15. A. Maurois, *Prometheus: Balzac's Life* (London: Bodley Head, 1965).

16. R.J. House and J.M. Howell, "Personality and Charismatic Leadership," *Leadership Quarterly* 3 (2) (1992): 81–108.

17. M. Popper and O. Neeman, *Characteristics of Personalized and Socialized Charismatic Leaders* (Submitted for publication.)

18. J. Bowlby, *A Secure Base: Clinical Applications of Attachment Theory*. (London: Routledge, 1988).

19. C. Darwin, *The Autobiography and Selected Letters* (New York: Dover, 1958).

20. K. Lorenz, *Evolution and Modification of Behavior* (London: Methuen, 1966).

21. H.F. Harlow, *Learning to Love* (San Francisco: Albion, 1973).

22. E. Berne, *Games People Play* (Hamondsworth, Middlesex: Penguin Books, 1972).

23. R. Harris, *I'm OK, You're OK* (New York: Avon, 1972).

24. K. Bartholomew and L.M. Horowitz, "Attachment Styles Among Young Adults: A Test of a Four-Category Model," *Journal of Personality and Social Psychology* 61 (1991): 226–244.

25. C. Hazan and P. Shaver, "Romantic Love Conceptualized as an Attachment Process," *Journal of Personality and Social Psychology* 52 (1987): 511–524.

26. O. Castelnovo, "Transformational Leadership and Attachment" (Master's MA thesis, University of Haifa, 1996). (In Hebrew)

27. A. Toffler, *Power Shift* (New York: Bantam Books, 1990).

28. Z.J. Lippowski, "Sensory and Information Inputs Overloaded: Behavioral Effects." *Comprehensive Psychiatry* 16 (1975): 199–221.

29. Lindholm, "Lovers and Leaders," 114.

30. L. Lasch, *The Minimal Self* (New York: Norton, 1984).

31. O. Kernberg, "Boundaries and Structure in Love Relationships," *Journal of the American Psychoanalytic Association* 25 (1977): 81–144.

32. S. Har-Even, "Four Models of Leadership" (Paper presented at a Seminar on Leadership, Open University, Tel Aviv, 1992). (In Hebrew)

33. Ibid.

Index

Adler, Alfred, 13
altered states of consciousness, 54, 55
attachment theory, 95, 96
attribution, 39
Aztec, 69

Balzac, Honoré de, 92
Beauvoir, Simone de, 88
Berne, Eric, 4, 95
borderline personality, 11
Bowlby, John, 94, 95, 96, 97
brainwashing, 53

charisma, 48, 65, 73, 89, 100–101
Chaplin, Charlie, 98
Churchill, Winston, xv, 22, 25, 49, 50, 90
cognitive dissonance, 57
collectivism, 70–71

Darwin, Charles, 94
Da Vinci, Leonardo, 31
defense mechanism, xi

delaying transference, 28
denial, xi, xiii, 59
Dionysus, 68
Durkheim, Emile, 65, 71

Eichmann, Adolf, 37
Einstein, Albert, 92
emotional intelligence, 64
Engels, Friedrich, 46, 88
espoused theory, 85

Faust, 75–78
field force theory, 55
"foot in the door, a," 58
Freud, Sigmund, xii, xiii, 13, 15, 19, 29, 31, 36–37, 52, 54, 65, 66
Fromm, Erich, xvi
fundamental attribution error, 39–40

Gabriel, 76
Gandhi, Mahatma, 19, 25, 32, 97
gestalt, 44
Goethe, 76, 78

"good enough mother," 17
Graham, Billy, 57, 58
grandiose self, 15–17, 19

Harlow, Harry F., 12, 30, 94
Hegel, Georg Friedrich, 89–90
Heine, Heinrich, 78
Herod, 99
Hitler, Adolf, x, xi, xiv, xv, xvii,
    10–11, 12, 18–19, 21, 25, 26, 29,
    44, 60, 63, 64, 79
Hugo, Victor, 89

identification with the aggressor,
    54
Iliad, 69
individualism, 69, 70, 71
individuation, 17–18
inferiority complex, 13

Jones, Jim, ix–x, xi, xiv, xv, 6–9, 11,
    12, 21, 26, 29, 59–60, 61, 62

Kernberg, Otto, 29, 101
Kohut, Heinz, 15–16, 20, 27, 37

Lewin, Kurt, 55, 62, 75
Lorenz, Konrad, 94
Luther, Martin, 32, 75, 76, 77, 78

Machiavellianism, 94
Mandela, Nelson, 97
Manson, Charles, xiv, xv, 1–6, 11,
    12, 20, 21, 25, 26, 31, 60, 62, 64
Marx, Karl, 46–47, 87, 88, 89
Maurois, André, 92
Maya, 69
Mephistopheles, 75, 76
mirroring, 14–17, 27
mirroring transference, 28

narcissistic deprivation, 27
New Testament, 69
Nietzsche, Friedrich, 78
Nirgihazy, Irvin, 91

Odyssey, 69
Old Testament, 69

personality disturbance, 12, 27
personalized charismatic leader,
    xviii, 27, 30, 93, 94, 98, 100
Phaeton complex, 24
power distance, 70, 72
primary narcissism, 29
primary processes, 54
Prometheus, 68
pure child, the, 4

rationalization, xi, 5, 57
regression, 29, 54
repression, xi
reprogramming, 4
Roosevelt, Franklin Delano, 63, 82,
    88

schoolboy pattern, 56
separation, 17, 18
socialized charismatic leader, xviii,
    27, 30, 93–94, 97
superego, 56

theory in practice, 85, 86
Third Reich, xix, 79
third wave, 98, 99
thought reform, 53–54
Toffler, Alvin, 98, 99
transactional leadership, 50–51
transformational leadership, 50–51
trauma, xv, 22, 24, 63–64
twice born, 18, 19

uncertainty avoidance, 69, 71, 72
Uriel, 76

Weber, Max, 47–48, 88
Wilson, Woodrow, xv, 14, 26, 32

yin and yang, 69

About the Author

MICHA POPPER is a lecturer in the Departments of Psychology and Education at the University of Haifa and a director of the Center for Outstanding Leadership. A former head of the School for Leadership Development of the Israel Defense Forces, Dr. Popper has published two earlier books and numerous articles on leadership issues.